GRE
Cram Course

GRE
Cram Course

Suzee J. Vlk

Prentice Hall
New York • London • Toronto • Sydney • Tokyo • Singapore

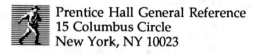

Prentice Hall General Reference
15 Columbus Circle
New York, NY 10023

An Arco Book

Arco, Prentice Hall, and colophons are
registered trademarks of Simon & Schuster, Inc.

Library of Congress Cataloging-in-Publication Data

Vlk, Suzee
  GRE cram course/ Suzee J. Vlk. —2nd ed.
      p.   cm.
  Rev. ed. of: GRE cram course/ Ronald G. Vlk. 1986.
  ISBN 0-671-84669-8
  1. Graduate Record Examination—Study guides. I. Vlk, Ronald G.
GRE cram course. II. Title.
LB2367.4.V55 1991
378.1′662—dc20   91-9581
                                                              CIP

Manufactured in the United States of America

3 4 5 6 7 8 9 10

CONTENTS

PREFACE

Why Use the 10-hour Plan?

There are many people who cannot or simply will not spend more than 10 hours studying for an exam. If you agree with one or more of the following statements, this book is just right for you.

1.   I am not certain whether or not I am actually going to take the GRE; I just want a book that I can browse through to determine what types of questions are on the exam and how hard they will be.

2.   I haven't decided whether to take the GRE and go for a Master's degree or even a Ph.D., take the GMAT and go for my MBA (master of business administration); or take the LSAT and go to law school. I want some books that are short enough to enable me to go through more than one to help me make my choice.

3.   I know I will be taking the GRE sometime, but I don't know when. I want a short book I can skim to help me determine whether I will need to take any special courses (such as more math) to prepare myself for taking the exam a few years down the road.

4.   I am the type who needs discipline and has trouble working without a specific study plan. This 10-hour format, with everything organized for me, will help me stick to my studies and not quit halfway through.

5.   I don't have a lot of money and really don't want to gamble the cost of a full-length test preparation book; however, I won't miss the few dollars spent on this book (even if for some reason I decide not to take the exam).

6.   I have a career and/or a family, which takes up much of my time. I want a short book that I can work through, not a long intimidating tome that will take more than I can or will give.

7.   I suddenly decided to take the GRE and was dismayed to find out that the exam is being given in just a few weeks/days. I don't have time to go through a lengthy study program; 10 hours sounds just right.

8.   I have already taken the GRE (or other exams somewhat similar to it) and don't think I need to do a great deal of studying again. All I need is a brief review that will tell me what similarities and differences this exam has from the other exam(s) I took.

9.   I have already taken a GRE preparation course (at school or through a private test preparation business). I feel I am prepared, but I want some sort of quick refresher.

10.   I just found out that test preparation books exist; I want to gain the maximum benefits from studying but only have a short time to do so.

Do any of the above statements sound familiar? Perhaps you found yourself making them to your family or friends, or muttering them to yourself as you stood in front of the many test preparation books displayed in a bookstore. This book is written for you, the person who wants to do the job quickly but well. To find out how to minimize the pain and maximize the gain, turn to the introduction where you will find the 10-hour plan explained in detail.

1.

DAY ONE

Hour One: Introduction to the 10-hour Study Plan and Overview of the GRE

Set Your Clock. You were promised a 10-hour study plan; a 10-hour study plan is what you will get. Your 10 hours begin now with your reading of this Introduction, your working through the exercises, and your getting a basic overview of the GRE—how it is organized, timed and scored. With the second hour, you plunge right into your study program and learn how to approach and handle some of the verbal ability questions.

This book has been very carefully designed to give you all the information you need in a concise format so that you can do an excellent job of studying for the GRE in just 10 hours. These 10 hours are to be broken up into five 2-hour sessions. NOTE: It is strongly suggested that you do indeed study in units of 2 hours at a time; however, some units are written so that you can break them up into 1-hour segments. For example, on Day One you could read this Introduction, work through the exercises, and learn about the structure of the GRE in one hour. You could, if absolutely necessary, do the second hour's worth of work on another day. The same thing applies with Day Two; if you absolutely had to, you could spend just one hour on the first segment (sentence completion and reading comprehension) then come back to the second hour and begin your math review on another day.

Exercise One: Setting Up Your Schedule

At the back of this book you will find a "calendar"; rip it out now and use it on this exercise. As you can see, the calendar is

1

a study organizer, a chart telling you what you will be studying on which day and for how long. This is only a suggested organization. You may, if you wish, change the order of the sections, with one exception. You *must* do the first hour's material (that is, this Introduction and Overview of the GRE) in the first hour. If you do not do so, you will be completely confused by subsequent instructions and information.

Take the time right now to fill in on your calendar exactly which days and which hours you will use to study. If at all possible, try to set aside the same hours every day. If you work, you may want to set aside 7:00 to 9:00 P.M. If you do not work, you may wish to study from 10:00 A.M. to noon daily. Whatever hours you choose, do try to use two hours in a row, at a time when you will not be disturbed by others. Using the same hours daily will help you stick to your schedule.

The following are some factors you should consider when planning your study schedule:

1. What hours may I set aside without feeling guilty for neglecting my family or my studies?

2. What hours may I set aside where I will not be disturbed (by children, friends, or co-workers)?

3. Will I be able to stick to those hours, even if they fall on a weekend or a holiday?

4. Am I fresh enough to study during those hours? (You may not want to study from 10:00 P.M. to midnight, after you are exhausted from a long day.)

5. Are my hours of study realistic? (Many persons swear to themselves that they will actually get up at 5:00 A.M. to study; such good intentions usually last one day at most!)

All right, you have now filled in your study schedule and are determined to stick to it. However, there probably will be some variations; how you deal with them will significantly affect your overall success on this study program.

Missing a Day. What happens if you become ill, or you have an obligation elsewhere, and cannot study on a particular day?

First of all, don't become overly concerned. Do not automatically assume that your study plan is ruined and that you may as well give up the whole thing. There are several alternatives you should consider.

1. *Make up the lost time on the same day.* If at all possible, the best way to make up the time is to set aside two hours (or at least one) on that *same day.* Even if you have to give up your favorite television program or your evening aerobics class, try to fit in your studying on that very day. Not only will you stick to your schedule somewhat, you will feel wonderfully virtuous.

2. *Make up the lost time by doubling up your study time on another day.* This means that instead of studying two hours on another day, you study four hours on that day. While this is not recommended, you may find that it is your only option. If you must put in four hours on one day, break them up as much as possible. Try to put in two hours in the morning and two in the evening. At the very least, take a half-hour break between the sessions; get up and walk around.

3. *Make up the lost time by adding another day on the end of your study schedule.* Of course, this is the optimum alternative; simply study Monday through Saturday instead of Monday through Friday. However, you may find that your schedule is too tight to allow you to do this.

4. *Skip a section entirely.* This is the last thing you want to do, but you may find it is your only alternative. If you absolutely cannot add another day to your study schedule, and you cannot study more than two hours a day, your only choice is to skip one day's worth of study. If that is your plan, by all means be careful to skip that day from which you would gain the least. You will have to make a personal decision whether you can best afford to neglect a verbal section (antonyms, analogies, sentence completion, or reading comprehension), a mathematical section (quantitative comparisons, problem solving, or data interpretation), or an analytical section (analytical reasoning or logical reasoning).

What you do *not* want to do is to skim through each section, trying to do everything in half the time. That is, do not try to cram two 2-hour sessions into only two hours. Each section has already been compacted as much as possible; setting out to do one in less than the recommended time is probably going to mean that rather than understanding one section entirely, you don't understand two sections at all.

Extra Time. What do you do if you have extra time? Maybe you will find that you enjoy studying this material and would like to have more. Maybe you will find that you have unexpectedly obtained more time (a kind boss gives you a day off; a teacher is ill, canceling classes). You should take advantage of your extra time in one of the following ways.

1. *Memorize key concepts and have a friend quiz you on them.* If you have extra time, you may be able to memorize more math rules. Most persons who have only 10 hours to study have to be content with understanding all the rules and memorizing the most important ones; with extra time you can go back and memorize all of the rules.

2. *Retake the short tests offered at the end of each section.* Answer *all* of the questions, not just the ones you missed the first time through. As you answer each question, ask yourself what concept it was testing, and what specific piece of information you needed to answer it. You may be pleasantly surprised later to find that questions on the actual GRE are very, very similar to questions found in these materials.

3. *Review outside materials.* Supplementary reading is to be done *only* if you have already completed all 10 hours of study. It is *supplementary*, meaning that it is in addition to your basic study plan. Do not spend time on supplementary materials in lieu of your regular study materials.

So far, so good. You have now set aside time for studying. You have some idea how to salvage the situation if you get behind in your studies, and how best to use any additional time you may have. You are ready for the last step in these introductory materials: the Preview.

Exercise Two: Previewing

To preview material is to skim through it, finding salient points. Take a few minutes now to go back and read the table of contents. See what this book has to offer. Now flip through the body of the book, seeing how it is set up. By doing so, you will be more comfortable with the material when you are actually ready to sit down and begin working on it. By the way, previewing is an excellent skill to develop and use on the actual GRE.

Overview of the GRE

The GRE is a seven-section exam, with all questions in the multiple choice format. There is no writing sample section (that is, you will not have to write an essay). The sections are as follows:

Verbal Ability	38 questions	30 minutes
Quantitative Ability	30 questions	30 minutes
Analytical Ability	25 questions	30 minutes

Duplication. Usually, each section is given *twice*. Although it is highly unlikely, it is possible that one section may be given only once, while another section is given three times. The sections are given in no particular order. Several editions of the exam are in use at any given time, so persons at the same testing site may not be taking exactly the same test. Scores are scaled to ensure fairness.

The Experimental Section. The seventh section is experimental ("seventh section" does not necessarily mean it is found in the seventh place on the exam). It does not count toward your final score. Generally, the experimental section is similar to one of the three basic types given above; you will not be able to determine which section is the experimental one. *Do your best on every section*, even if you think you know which section is experimental. Perhaps you feel the questions in one section are significantly more difficult than the questions in another section, giving you the feeling that, "This section *must* be the experimental one." You could be right, but then again, you could be wrong.

Further details and information on each question type will be given in the section dealing with that question.

Determination of Your Score

On the GRE, you receive a point for every question you answer correctly. You receive no points for any questions you simply do not answer. Here's the good news: There is no penalty for wrong answers. In other words, if you guess and miss, you lose no points. Therefore, it is obviously to your advantage to guess, even if you have absolutely no idea of the correct answer. *Never* leave an answer blank. This is different from scoring on other exams (for example, on the GMAT you are penalized ¼ point for every wrong answer).

NOTE: The above scoring information only applies to the GRE General Test. It does not apply to the subject tests (the advanced tests in specific subjects, such as biology or chemistry). You *are* penalized for incorrect answers on the subject tests.

To determine your score, give yourself one point for each question you answered correctly. This number is known as your *Raw Score*. Before the score reports are sent to you or your designated schools, the raw score is converted to a *Scaled Score*. This is a score on a common scale used for all editions of the test. The scaled score allows for a fair comparison among test takers who were given various editions of the GRE, some of which might be considered easier than others. The scaled score reflects approximately the same level of ability regardless of the edition of the test that was taken.

For the General Test, you will receive separate scores for verbal, quantitative, and analytical ability. The minimum score reported is 200; even if you answer no questions in that section or answer all the questions incorrectly, a score of 200 will be reported for you. (NOTE: Again, this information is different for the subject tests. If you are going to take a subject test, you may want to write to the Educational Testing Service (ETS) and request its information booklet that specifically relates to your particular exam or exams.)

All GRE scores are given in three digits and end in 0. Typical scores could be 620, 690, or 740. The highest possible score is an 800.

The Score Report

Approximately four to six weeks after you have taken the exam, you will be sent a score report. This is simply a small piece of paper giving separate verbal, quantitative, and analytical ability scores. With the exception of the analytical ability scores, score reports will also state *percentile* ranks. Such ranks indicate how your scores compare to those of others taking the same exam.

Using the Scores

When you apply to take the GRE, you will be asked to which schools you want your scores to be sent. Your scores will be sent automatically to those schools at the same time they are sent to you. No scores will be released without your written permission.

If you take the exam more than once, the three most recent scores will be sent to the designated schools. You *cannot* ask to have a school sent only your highest score.

Individual schools vary greatly in the manner in which they use the GRE score. Some schools give it the same weight as your grade point average (GPA). Some schools use it almost exclusively to determine who will be admitted. A few schools use it only in the case of your being a "borderline" applicant. You definitely should write or call your school before taking the GRE to find out how important your test score will be to your application. NOTE: Chances are you will be applying to more than one school. Do not assume that all schools have the same policy, or that you will get into the school of your choice. Contact each school.

Scoring Errors

Since all exams are scored electronically, it is highly unlikely that an error will be made on the grading of your exam. However, if you feel that such an error has been made, you may ask to have your exam hand graded. When you receive your score report, included with it will be a form which you may complete and return—along with the specified fee—to the address given on the form. You must make such a rescoring request within 120 days of the postmark on the score report.

You will receive the results of the hand grading within approximately four weeks of receipt of your request. If the hand grading shows a different result from the electronic scoring, the hand graded results will be sent to all designated recipients of the earlier scores.

Repeating the Exam

You may repeat the GRE as often as you like. The exam is given several times a year; if you want to repeat it, you may, but you will have to pay a fee each time.

Schools vary in their consideration of multiple scores. Some schools look only at your highest score. Some schools average all the scores. Some schools look at your highest score, but subtract points from it for each time you repeated the exam. Again, call or write your school directly. NOTE: Even within the same college or university, different programs may have different ways of using the scores. Try to talk to the person who would be your department head.

For More Information

This has been a brief overview of the exam. If you want more specific information, read the *GRE Information Bulletin*. This is a small pamphlet distributed free by ETS (Educational Testing Service). You may obtain a copy of the bulletin at most colleges and universities with graduate programs. If there is not a college or university near you, write to ETS at:

Graduate Record Examinations
CN 6000
Princeton, New Jersey 08541-6000

NOTE: The bulletin discussed above is also the *Applications Bulletin*; chances are you already have one. There is a lot of information in that bulletin that you may not need (such as registering to take the exam if you are overseas); you may not have the time to go through it entirely. If you decide to take the GRE, you will need it for the application forms and envelope bound inside.

Hour Two: Verbal Ability (Part I)

Set Your Clock. *You will have a full hour to learn about the first two (out of four) question types found in the verbal ability section of the GRE. These questions are antonyms and analogies. The remaining two verbal question types, sentence completion and reading comprehension, will be covered in the first hour tomorrow.*

What You Will See

The Verbal Ability section has 38 questions. Generally, eleven of those are antonyms and nine are analogies.

Antonyms. Each antonym question consists of two parts: the word being tested and five answer choices. The word being tested will be printed in all capital letters; the answer choices will be in lower case letters.

EXAMPLE: LISTLESS: A. restless B. energetic C. creative
D. uneducated E. rude

Analogies. Each analogy question consists of two parts: the test pair of words and the five answer pairs. The test pair of words will be printed in all capital letters; the answer choices will be in lower case letters.

EXAMPLE: HAIRY:BALD:: A. tall:slender B. female:feminine
C. slovenly:messy D. ecstatic:miserable
E. successful:wealthy

Ordering the Questions

In the verbal section, generally the antonyms and analogies are not the first two question types. In fact, it is not uncommon to find the antonyms at the very end of the section. Often the order of the questions is as follows: sentence completion, analogies, reading comprehension, antonyms. *Regardless of the order in which the question types are presented, do the antonyms first.* Answering an antonym question takes very little time. You only have to read a total of six words. In the time that it would take you to read one reading comprehension question, or one sentence completion question, you could read and answer all 11 antonyms. Therefore, by doing the antonyms first, you are making the wisest use of your time.

NOTE: Some people feel that the antonyms are the most difficult question type because they test vocabulary knowledge. Even if you feel your vocabulary is weak, do the antonyms *first*. If you miss one, or two, or several, at least you tried. Remember there is no penalty for incorrect answers on the GRE. If you leave "those hard antonyms" for the end of the section, you might not have time to answer them, or even to take a guess. If you don't fill in any answer, you have no chance of getting a point.

After you have done the antonyms, answer the analogy questions. With the analogies, you only have to read 12 words. You could finish all of the analogies in the time it would take you to do just a few reading comprehension or sentence completion questions.

NOTE: Be very careful when you skip around within a section to keep track of your answers in the proper spaces on your answer grid. If you are doing antonyms which are questions 28–38, be certain you are filling in answer ovals 28–38, not 1–11.

How to Do the Questions

Antonyms. With an antonym question, you should do the following:

1. *Read the question word.* This seems obvious and simple, but you must be careful of one thing: read the word that is actually printed, not the word you want to see. For example, you may see the word "designated" but accidentally read "designed." When you go to look for an antonym, you may become totally confused and frustrated because there is no word that means the opposite of "designed." Then, after becoming irritated and wasting pre-

cious time trying to force one of the answers to meet your needs, you have to go back and reread the word as it should have been read the first time. Take your time reading each question.

2. *Define the question word.* Before you look at the answer choices, ask yourself what the question word means. For example, if the word is "listless," you know that it means "lethargic, lacking energy, slow-moving." Don't worry about finding "precise" definitions; the only one who knows what you are thinking is yourself. If the word is an adjective but you define it as a noun, that's fine, as long as you get the general meaning. If you can't think of an exact definition, but have a hazy idea of what the word means from having seen it used in some context, fine. How you define the word is up to you. Just do take the time to think about what the word means *before* going on to the next step.

3. *Predict the answer.* An antonym is a word meaning "opposite." When you are looking for an antonym, you are looking for a word that means the opposite of your question word. Since you have already defined listless to yourself, you can go ahead and predict a word that is the opposite. If you defined listless as "lacking energy," it is a simple step to predict that an opposite is "having energy," or "energetic." Again, don't worry about finding exactly the right word or exactly the right form; simply get a general idea of what a possible antonym would be.

4. *Look for the answer.* Now that you have predicted that the answer is "energetic," read the answer choices to determine whether that exact answer or one similar in meaning to it is given. If you note the example given earlier in this section, "energetic" is answer choice B. By defining the word and predicting its opposite, you have taken the quickest and most accurate route to obtaining an answer.

5. *Check your answer.* Most of the time, the word you *predict* as an antonym will in fact be given in the answer key and will be the correct answer. The vast majority of the time you may feel confident that your prediction is correct; trust yourself. However, if you are uncertain of your definition, or you have a little extra time, you may want to read the other four answer choices to be absolutely certain that there is no other answer that is a little

"more correct," one that seems to be a slightly better opposite. For example, if you were looking for the opposite of white, gray would be right, but black would be "more right." Generally, however, you do *not* want to spend a lot of time thinking about all of the answer choices. If you have predicted an answer that is given as an answer choice, you should go on to the next question.

What Do I Do When . . . ?

Suppose that you have followed all of the steps above very carefully. You took your time reading the word so that you didn't make a careless error. You defined the word, predicted its antonym, and looked at the answer key, only to find there is no answer there remotely resembling what you had hoped to find! Now what?

Now you do two things. First, you *review your question.* Go back and reread the question word to make absolutely certain you read it correctly. Redefine it in your mind, to make certain that you used a good definition. Try to remember where, in what context, you have seen the word used. Predict an answer again. Check the answer choices again. *Be certain that you are matching the right answer choices to the right question word.* Occasionally, a student will read question 36 but look at the answer choices for question 37. Be very careful not to make such careless errors.

If you are positive you have made no "technical" errors, the next step is to *use the answer choices.* Read all five of the answer choices. If two or more words are synonyms (words that mean the same thing), *both* those words must be wrong. This is because two answers cannot be correct; therefore, neither one is correct. This will help you eliminate two out of the five answers.

Next, try to look at the prefixes of the words. Although you may be tricked by prefixes once in a while (for example, you may find a word that begins with "mal" meaning "bad" is in fact not the opposite of a word that begins with "bene," meaning "good,") it is generally helpful to pay attention to prefixes.

Finally, if all else fails, *guess.* Don't hesitate to make a guess because there are no penalty points on this exam. If you have never seen the word before, if you have absolutely no idea what it means, guess right away and go on to the next question. Don't waste any time on a word with which you are completely unfamiliar.

Analogies. With an analogy question you should do the following:

1. *Read the question words.* As with the antonyms, take the time to read the words that are actually printed. Do not subconsciously substitute words of your own.

2. *Find the relationship between the question words.* This step is the heart of the entire analogies process. An analogy is a comparison between two things, a likening of one thing to another. When you see an analogy, ask yourself what the *relationship* is between the items. Is one a part of the other? Did one occur earlier in time than the other? Does one follow the other? If you properly define the relationship between the items, you will get the correct answer.

There are several basic relationships that are found on this exam. While these are by no means all of the relationships that may be tested, many questions use these.

PART–WHOLE

EXAMPLE: QUESTION:EXAM. A question is a part or portion of an exam.

EXAMPLE: STEM:FLOWER. A stem is a part of a flower.

COMPONENT–PRODUCT

EXAMPLE: BUTTER:CAKE. Butter is a component, an ingredient of a cake (the cake is the product).

EXAMPLE: CHIP:COMPUTER. A chip is a component of a computer (the computer is the product).

SYNONYMS

EXAMPLE: HAIRY:HIRSUTE. To be hairy or covered with hair is the same as to be hirsute.

EXAMPLE: ARROGANT:HAUGHTY. To be arrogant or conceited is the same as to be haughty.

ANTONYMS

EXAMPLE: LANGUID:FRENETIC. To be languid is to be listless, nonenergetic. To be frenetic is to be very energetic, active.

EXAMPLE: KNOTTY:SIMPLE. To be knotty is to be difficult and complex (such as a knotty problem); the opposite of simple.

CAUSE-EFFECT

EXAMPLE: OVEREAT:OBESITY. To overeat is to become obese (fat); overeating is the cause, obesity is the result or effect.

EXAMPLE: SABOTAGE:DISASTER. To sabotage something is to harm or hinder it, possibly leading to disaster.

CHARACTERISTIC

EXAMPLE: WATER:POTABLE. Water has the characteristic of being potable (drinkable).

EXAMPLE: CLICHÉ:HACKNEYED. A cliché, a statement or saying that has been overused, has the characteristic of being hackneyed, of being trite or lacking in originality and freshness.

PROGRESSION

EXAMPLE: JUNIOR:SENIOR. A junior who performs well in school progresses to becoming a senior.

EXAMPLE: BOY:MAN. A boy becomes a man.

3. *Choose the answer with the same relationship.* Once you have determined the relationship between the words in the question, look

for a pair of words in the answers that has that same relationship. Note that the *meanings* of the words are irrelevant. If the question words are about baboons but have the relationship of cause-effect, it makes no difference that the answer words are about scientists. As long as the *relationship* is correct, your answer is correct.

What Do I Do When . . . ?

If you have followed the preceding steps but cannot seem to find a correct answer, go back through the same steps again. Much, if not most of the time, the problem lies in sheer carelessness. Did you read the question words incorrectly? Did you choose the wrong relationship? Did you look at the answers to the wrong question? Take the time to go back through the process one more time.

If you cannot find the relationship between the words in the question because you don't know what those words mean, guess at an answer and go on. Don't waste your time trying to analyze an answer. For example, suppose the question words are IRASCI-BLE:CHOLERIC. If you don't know what even one of the words (let alone both!) means, there is no way you can find an answer. As far as you know they could be synonyms (true: each means grouchy, irritable), antonyms, or virtually anything else.

Traps to Avoid

With antonyms, there are three basic traps to avoid:

1. *Do not misread the word.* As discussed earlier, it is very, very easy to transpose a few letters and, for example, make "angle" out of "angel." Take the time to read the question word carefully.

2. *Remember to choose an antonym.* Many persons who make mistakes in this section do so because they defined the word, then looked for that definition among the answer choices. You want an *opposite,* not a synonym. Often you will find that synonyms *are* given as answer choices; don't let them trap you.

3. *Keep track of your numbering.* With these short questions, it is easy to make numerical mistakes twice, once on the questions

(where you read question 36 but the answers for question 37) and once on the answer grid (where you fill in ovals 1–11, rather than 28–38).

With analogy questions, there are three basic traps to avoid:

1. *Do not misread the words.* Unfortunately, people tend to read the first word, then predict the second word. For example, if the first word is "man," many people think that the second word must be "woman." They play "word association" games, rather than reading the question. Take the time to do a careful reading.

2. *Do not choose an answer with a reversed relationship.* This is perhaps the most common error in this section. If the question is BOY:MAN, the answer *cannot* be WOMAN:GIRL. The relationship would be one of progression; a boy grows into a man. A woman does not grow into a girl; the relationship there is reversed.

3. *Do not choose answers based on the meanings of the words.* If the questions are about computers, the answer may very easily be about chocolate cake. The *meanings* themselves are irrelevant; you are only concerned with the *relationships* between the pairs of words.

Time-saving Suggestions

Antonyms

1. *Do the antonyms first.* Each antonym only requires a few seconds to read and answer.

2. *Predict and look for an answer.* You save much time if you already have an idea of what you are looking for, rather than just moseying through the answer choices. Once you find the answer you have predicted, you may go on to the next question. You really don't have to look through the rest of the answers unless you are unsure of your definition, or you have extra time.

3. *Guess with impunity.* If you have absolutely no idea what a word means, don't worry and fret over it, trying to analyze it. Un-

less you know that the meaning is on the tip of your tongue, so to speak, don't think about it. With antonyms, either you know them immediately, or you don't.

Analogies

1. *Do the analogies second.* Each analogy should only take you a few seconds to read and answer.

2. *Define the relationship as quickly as possible.* If you have memorized the relationships given above, you will find that many problems will demonstrate one of them. If the question words do not fit neatly into a specific relationship, create your own with a sentence, such as ESKIMO:SUNBURN. "An Eskimo is *unlikely* to get sunburn."

3. *Guess with impunity.* As always, if you have no idea what one or both of the words mean, choose an answer and go on to the next question. Do not waste your time trying to analyze it, or staring at it as if the meaning of a word you have never seen before will suddenly pop into your mind. If the word is familiar (you have seen it before but can't quite remember what it means), then it might be worth a moment of thought. However, if you didn't even know that such a word existed ("multifariousness?!"), go on to the next question.

Practice Exam: Antonyms and Analogies

Please take the following practice exam on antonyms and analogies. The verbal ability section of the actual exam has 38 questions; these 11 antonyms and nine analogies are representative of a portion of that section. Read the directions and answer the questions. Explanatory answers follow the answer key. Score yourself, giving yourself one point for each correct answer. Do *not* subtract points for wrong answers.

Antonyms

DIRECTIONS: Each question consists of a word printed in capital letters and five words printed in lower case letters. Choose the word or group of words that is most nearly *opposite* in meaning to the word printed in capital letters. Circle the letter that appears before your choice.

1. ARBITRARY: A. unplanned B. deliberate C. mature D. hackneyed E. boring

2. GOAD: A. refuse B. anticipate C. disparage D. discourage E. glower

3. INNATE: A. acquired B. obtuse C. slender D. knotty E. discordant

4. DILATORY: A. shrunken B. accelerating C. arbitrary D. derisive E. simple

5. CRYPTIC: A. languid B. approbatory C. feminine D. spacious E. obvious

6. GRATUITOUS: A. costly B. unexpected C. habitable D. separate E. equivocal

7. LAMENTABLE: A. ridiculous B. slow C. fortunate D. mandatory E. overbearing

8. SECTARIAN: A. universal B. religious C. threadbare D. exaggerated E. free

9. WHET: A. dull B. open C. verify D. silence E. urge

10. TORPID: A. numb B. sluggish C. vigorous D. masculine E. tentative

11. DIATRIBE: A. paean B. critique C. criticism D. ridicule E. comparison

Analogies

DIRECTIONS: Each question consists of a pair of words printed in capital letters and five pairs of words printed in lower case letters. Find the relationship between the words printed in capital letters.

Then choose from among the words printed in lower case letters that pair which most nearly has the same relationship. Circle the letter that appears before your answer.

1. NOVICE : TYRO :: A. expert:beginner B. singer:vocalist C. dictator:subject D. government:elections E. student: professor

2. THREADBARE : NEW :: A. eroded:diminished B. unclothed:naked C. obese:emaciated D. ancient:antique E. disheveled:slovenly

3. WATERLOGGED : FLOOD :: A. refrigerator:cold B. car:speedy C. warm:sunshine D. liquid:fluid E. ocean:waves

4. CLASP : NECKLACE :: A. knob:door B. law:government C. bracelet:wrist D. belt:buckle E. head:neck

5. MILK : BUTTER :: A. cow:bull B. skim:whole C. batter:cake D. ice:water E. beginning:conclusion

6. ANIMALS : FUR :: A. humans:skin B. men:hair C. women: clothing D. monsters:slime E. scales:fish

7. CRYPTIC : BAFFLING :: A. mysterious:obvious B. innate: acquired C. approbatory:disapproving D. gusty:still E. chaotic:confusing

8. RATTLE : BOTTLE :: A. bone:collar B. trousers:slacks C. baby:adult D. books:professor E. shake:burp

9. RAIN : DELUGE :: A. desert:dry B. duck:swim C. tremor: earthquake D. gust:breeze E. precipitation:rainfall

ANTONYMS ANSWER KEY

1. B	4. B	7. C	10. C
2. D	5. E	8. A	11. A
3. A	6. A	9. A	

Explanations

1. **(B)** *Arbitrary* means selected at random and without reason; discretionary. "Peter made an *arbitrary* choice of a movie,

moving his finger down the list with his eyes closed." The opposite is deliberate, which means planned.

2. **(D)** *Goad* means to incite or rouse; to impel. "His friends were finally able to *goad* him into riding on the roller coaster known as Killer." The opposite is to discourage, to try to convince not to do such an action.

3. **(A)** *Innate* means belonging to an individual from birth; inherent. "Only Luigi's *innate* sense of direction prevented the group from becoming hopelessly lost when the compass broke." The opposite is acquired, gained at a later date.

4. **(B)** *Dilatory* means tending to cause delay; slow. "Terry's *dilatory* tactics were appreciated by his fellow students who hoped that the bell would ring before a quiz could be given." The opposite is accelerating, tending or causing to occur more rapidly.

5. **(E)** *Cryptic* means vague; indistinct or mysterious. "The professor was mystified by the *cryptic* writings on the cave wall." The opposite is obvious, readily known, apparent.

6. **(A)** *Gratuitous* means costing nothing; free. "A smile is a *gratuitous* gesture that can make others happy without making your financial manager unhappy." The opposite is costly, expensive.

7. **(C)** *Lamentable* means regrettable, grievous, deplorable. "Sally's *lamentable* performance at the meet cost her a chance to go on to the finals next week." The opposite is fortunate, praiseworthy.

8. **(A)** *Sectarian* means limited in character or scope; parochial. "The *sectarian* school I attended did not adequately prepare me for the rigors of university life." The opposite is universal, all-encompassing.

9. **(A)** *Whet* means to make keen or more acute; to excite or sharpen. "Watching the Kentucky Derby *whets* Bill's appetite for horse racing." The opposite is to make dull, to make less intense.

10. **(C)** *Torpid* means having lost the power of exertion or feeling; numb. "The *torpid* python had just begun digesting a rabbit he had swallowed for his dinner." The opposite is vigorous, full of life, active.

11. **(A)** A *diatribe* is a bitter and abusive speech, a tirade. "The fiery minister delivered a *diatribe* on the evils of drinking." The opposite is a paean, which is a song of praise or joy.

ANALOGIES ANSWER KEY

1. B	4. A	6. A	8. A
2. C	5. C	7. E	9. C
3. C			

Explanations

1. **(B)** A *novice* and a *tyro* are the same thing; they are beginners. The relationship is one of synonyms; you are to look for two other words that mean the same thing. A singer is the same as a vocalist. Do not be trapped with answer A just because the word "beginner" is used. An expert would be considered the *opposite* of a beginner, so the relationship between the words is incorrect.

2. **(C)** *Threadbare* signifies that something is so old that it has become almost worn out. Clothing with sleeves that are almost worn through is called threadbare. The relationship is one of opposites; you need to look for two answer words that are opposites. *Obese* means very fat; *emaciated* means very skinny.

3. **(C)** Something that is *waterlogged* is full of water, sopping wet. It may have been in a flood. You want to find an answer choice where the first word is a condition that occurs because of the second word. "Something is *waterlogged* when it has been in a *flood*." The correct answer has this relationship: "Something is *warm* when it has been in the *sunshine*." You should not have chosen answer E just because all the words have to do with water. You want to use the relationships between the words, not the meanings of the words. Note that answer A has the correct relationship, but is in reverse order.

4. **(A)** A *clasp* is a part of a necklace; it is the fastener. The relationship is part to whole. A knob is a part of a door. If you chose answer C, you focused on the meaning of the words rather than on the relationship; a bracelet is not part of a wrist. If you chose answer D, you didn't notice that the relationship is reversed. A belt is not part of a buckle; a buckle is a part of a belt.

5. **(C)** This is a type of progression relationship. *Milk* is changed into *butter*. Batter is changed into cake. If you chose answer B, you were looking at the meanings of the words rather than the relationship between them. Answer D *could* be correct, but the order is usually reversed. (You think of water being turned to ice, not ice being turned to water.)

6. **(A)** This is a type of part–whole relationship. A part of an *animal*, its covering, is *fur*. The covering part of a human is skin. Note that answer E would be correct if it were reversed.

7. **(E)** *Cryptic* means baffling, confusing, mysterious. The words are synonyms. Chaotic means confusing, disorganized. If you chose answer A, you used the meaning of the words rather than the relationship. Mysterious and obvious are opposites, antonyms not synonyms.

8. **(A)** This is an example of an association analogy; a *rattle* and a *bottle* are characteristically associated with a baby. A bone and a collar are characteristically associated with a dog. If you chose answer E, you used the meanings of the words rather than their relationship.

9. **(C)** This is a progression relationship. A *deluge* is an overwhelming amount of rain, a flood. The correct answer has the same progression; a tremor (a small shaking of the earth) is much less than an earthquake. Answer D would be correct but is backwards (a gust is stronger than a breeze).

SCORE: NUMBER RIGHT:

NO PENALTY FOR WRONG ANSWERS

2.

DAY TWO

Hour One: Verbal Ability (Part II)

Set Your Clock. *You will have a full hour to learn about sentence completion and reading comprehension questions. In the second hour today, you will begin intensive math review.*

What You Will See

The Verbal Ability section has 38 questions. Generally, seven of those are sentence completion and eleven are reading comprehension questions.

Sentence Completion. Each sentence completion question consists of a full sentence with one or two blanks. Following the sentence are five answer choices containing a word or words to fit in the blank or blanks.

EXAMPLE: Although her doctor recommended that she _____ from talking so much, Frances was unable to _____ calling her best friend to tell her all the details of her date.

A. abstain . . . resist   D. refrain . . . halt
B. stop . . . eschew   E. keep . . . be
C. desist . . . stop

Reading Comprehension. Each reading comprehension "question" consists of two parts: the reading comprehension passage and a specific question based on information given or implied in that particular passage. Following is an example of just such a question; examples of the reading passages will be given in the practice exam later in these materials.

EXAMPLE: According to the passage, which of the following is true of Mount Klyuchevskaya?

A. It is in the capital city of Siberia.
B. It is in the central Siberian highlands.
C. It has the highest elevation of any place in Siberia.
D. It is the highest mountain in Russia.
E. All of the above.

Ordering the Questions. You learned in the last hour's lesson that you should do the antonyms first, then the analogies. After you have done those two question types, you should do the sentence completion and reading comprehension questions. Therefore, regardless of the actual order of the questions in the section, you should answer them in the following order:

- Antonyms
- Analogies
- Sentence Completion
- Reading Comprehension

You should do the sentence completion questions third because they require some time to read and think about. You have to read a complete sentence (as opposed to just a word or two words in the antonym and analogy questions) and think about it as an entity, try to make sense of it. Then you have to read the answer choices, and consider how well or poorly they would fit into the sentence. This often means that you end up reading the sentence several times, once with each answer choice inserted. Since this is relatively time consuming, save it for near the end.

NOTE: Because the sentence completion questions are familiar and comfortable (these are the type of "fill in the blank" questions you probably have seen throughout your academic career), you may be tempted to do them first. You may even feel that since you can get most of these right, and may not do nearly so well on the antonyms, these are your first priority. You may be correct that in terms of *percentages* you do the best on these. However, in the time it takes you to do one or two sentence completion questions, you could have done *all* of the antonyms and some of the analogies. Even if you miss several of those questions, your overall score is better than it would be with just the sentence completion questions. Therefore, force yourself to do the sentence completion questions *after* the antonyms and analogies.

The reading comprehension questions definitely should be done last. Each question takes significantly longer to do than does any question of any other type. You have to read the entire passage, then read the question, then *read all the answer choices* (because reading comprehension questions often have answers such as "all of the above" or "none of the above"). Doing all of this takes quite a while. If you begin with the reading comprehension questions, you may never get to some of the other questions. If you begin with the other questions, you may not be able to finish one or two reading comprehension questions—as opposed to all 11 of the antonyms or all nine of the analogies.

NOTE: Be *very* careful when you skip around within a section to keep track of your answers in the proper spaces on your answer grid. If you are doing sentence completion questions which are questions 1–7, be certain that you are filling in answer ovals 1–7, not 21–27.

How to Do the Questions

Sentence Completions. With a sentence completion question, you should do the following:

1. *Read the entire sentence through before looking at the answers.* Read the sentence to yourself, saying "blank" where the space is. In other words, you would say, "Although her doctor recommended that she *blank* from talking so much, Frances was unable to *blank* calling her best friend to tell her all the details of her date." If you read the answer words before you read the sentence or try to read them in conjunction with your first reading of the sentence, you will confuse yourself. Try to get the sense of the sentence first.

2. *Predict what words will fill in the blanks.* If you have read the sentence through and understood the gist of it, you should be able to *predict* what word or words will fit it. Don't spend a great deal of time trying to predict an exact word; just get the general idea, the connotation, of what is needed.

3. *Look for your prediction.* Very, very often you will find that the words you predicted are in the answer choices. Much of the time

your predictions will be exactly correct. If the words you predicted are not given, look for their synonyms.

4. *Check your answer.* You *must* go back and reread the *entire* sentence with your choice inserted. This step *cannot* be eliminated. If you reread the entire sentence, you will catch any errors or traps given. If you do not, you may later find that the first blank was correctly filled but that the second one confused the sentence entirely.

Reading Comprehension. With a reading comprehension question, you should do the following:

1. *Preview the passages.* Take just a few seconds to skim through the first and last paragraphs of *all* the passages. This brief reading will allow you to determine the passage *type* to which each belongs. You will probably encounter at least one example of each of the three basic types of reading passages: detail or factual (in which many specific facts or statistics are given), chronological (in which a progression of events is discussed), and theoretical (in which a theory is advanced or a hypothesis discussed).

2. *Order your passages.* You may find that you are better at reading, understanding, and answering questions on one type of passage than on another. For example, you may find that you are very good at "reading between the lines" and understanding theories, but that you cannot stand to read a dry passage filled with dates and numbers. In such a case, you would read and answer questions on a theoretical passage first, and save a detailed or factual passage for the end. By ordering the passage types you help yourself do those you are best in first. Thus, if you run out of time, you have left only those questions which you least enjoy and probably would have done the worst on anyway.

3. *Read and notate the passages.* You do *not* want to do a great deal of underlining and circling; you are not going to have to come back and take a semester final on this material someday! You will have the material right in front of you, to refer to as you go through the questions. However, if, as you read through a passage, you want to circle a particular definition which you think may be asked about, or you want to number the steps in a

progression, doing so will not take more than a few seconds. Remember that once you begin underlining, you may find that *everything* looks important, and that you are underlining almost the entire passage. If you are generally the underlining type, you may try to satisfy your urges by instead simply making short notes in the margin on the important point of each paragraph.

4. *Read each question and all of the answer choices.* Do *not* be tricked into choosing the first answer that seems right. Take the time to read *all* the answer choices because the question might have a later answer that says, "all of the above," or "answers A, C, and D" or something of that sort.

5. *Answer the question based on the preceding passage only.* Do not use information given in one passage to answer questions following a second passage; you may only use information from the passage directly before the questions. Do not use outside information, knowledge that you have yourself. If you do not remember the answer to the question, go back to the passage and look for it. If the question calls for you to make an inference (such as asking you what the tone of the author is), don't waste time going back to the passage (the answer won't be there). Instead, think about your answer for a moment, and choose the most likely choice given. Don't agonize too much over your choice on any given problem; go on to the next question.

Traps to Avoid

With the sentence completion questions, there are three basic traps to avoid.

1. *Don't read the answers before reading the sentence;* doing so will confuse you and prejudice your choice. Take the time to read the sentence through carefully and predict the answer.

2. *Don't stop after reading just one blank.* In other words, if there are two blanks to be filled, and the first word in the answer correctly fills the first one, don't automatically assume that that answer is correct. Frequently, answer choices do fill one blank correctly but fill the second blank incorrectly. Read and think about *both* words.

3. *Don't go on to the next question immediately after choosing your answer.* You must take the time to reread the entire sentence with your answer choice words filled in. This last step is one that persons tend to skip "in the interest of time," only to find out later that they made ridiculous and careless errors that could have been easily prevented.

With the reading comprehension questions, there are three basic traps to avoid.

1. *Use only information given in the immediately preceding passage.* Assume that whatever the passage states is correct (even if you know or believe the information to be incorrect or outdated) and answer your questions based on it. Do not read more into the passage than is printed there.

2. *Be certain you answer exactly what the question is calling for.* If the question asks you who was the first person to explore Australia, do not tell who was the first person to explore Austria. It is often easy to misread the question and give a "correct" answer to an "incorrect" question.

3. *Give the best answer.* Occasionally (especially on questions that call for deductions), you will find more than one "correct" answer. Choose the one that is "most correct." This means that you *must read all the answer choices* even if you think the first one you read could be correct.

Time-saving Suggestions

Sentence Completions

1. *Do the sentence completion questions third.* These questions take much longer than the antonyms and analogies, but not as long as the reading comprehension questions.

2. *Predict and look for an answer.* You save much time if you already have an idea of what you are looking for. Once you find the answer you have predicted, quickly insert it into the sentence to double check it. You will be pleasantly surprised to find out how often you have predicted *exactly* the right answer.

3. *Guess with impunity.* If you have absolutely no idea what answer to choose (for example, perhaps all the answers are words you have never seen before!), don't worry and fret over the sentence. Choose an answer and go on to the next question. Don't waste time looking through your answer grid to see whether you have "too many As and not enough Es," because the random ordering of questions and answers makes doing so useless.

Reading Comprehension

1. *Preview all the passages first.* This will allow you to know which passage to read first and which to save until the end.

2. *Do not do much underlining or circling.* If you want to make a special note, write a brief comment in the margin so that you can find a particular definition or point later if you are asked about it.

3. *Guess with impunity.* Since the reading comprehension portion of this section will be done last, you may find that you don't have time even to read a particular passage, let alone read, think about, and answer questions. Since there is no penalty for guessing, by all means fill in *something.* Even if you have only five seconds left, you can fill in a few ovals. If you fill in an oval, you at least have a chance.

Practice Exam: Sentence Completion and Reading Comprehension

Please take the following practice exam on sentence completion and reading comprehension. The "Verbal Ability" section of the actual exam has 38 questions; these seven sentence completion and eleven reading comprehension questions are representative of a portion of that section. Explanatory answers follow the answer key. Score yourself, giving yourself one point for each correct answer. Do not subtract points for wrong answers.

Sentence Completion

DIRECTIONS: Each sentence below has one or two blanks indicating omissions of words or phrases. Choose the word or group of words from the five answer choices that *best* fits the meaning of the sentence. Circle the letter that appears before your choice.

1. When the young man saw the _____ woman across the room, he ran over to be the first to ask her to dance.

   A. alluring   D. jejune
   B. childish   E. unsophisticated
   C. puerile

2. The arrogance of the actor was wholly _____ as he was just a _____ and had not yet earned the right to be conceited.

   A. expected . . . tyro   D. futile . . . fool
   B. unwarranted . . . beginner   E. ludicrous . . . thespian
   C. ridiculous . . . veteran

3. Although she admitted to having made a(n) _____ on the playing field, Gabriella still _____ that she had almost single-handedly won the game for her team.

   A. goal . . . said   D. shot . . . asserted
   B. mistake . . . denied E. error . . . refused
   C. blunder . . . maintained

4. The _____ remarks of the seemingly mature young man _____ his appearance and assured us that he was a callow youth after all.

   A. sophisticated . . . supported   D. inane . . . belied
   B. foolish . . . reinforced   E. charming . . . denied
   C. intelligent . . . mitigated

5. Because Alan had spoken so _____ of his ex-wife, we were all surprised to meet such a _____ young lady.

   A. disparagingly . . . charming   D. scathingly . . . contemptible
   B. glowingly . . . adorable   E. little . . . tall
   C. rudely . . . boorish

6. No one can succeed merely by _____ those who are already successful; one must have some virtues of one's own.

   A. reading about   D. watching
   B. emulating
   C. denying   E. hearing about

7. The convicts decided to _____ their escape plans when they agreed that the route through the desert was not _____.

   A. implement . . . easy   D. publicize . . . possible
   B. drop . . . hard   E. eschew . . . impossible
   C. postpone . . . feasible

Reading Comprehension

DIRECTIONS: Each passage is followed by questions pertaining to that passage. Read the passage and answer the questions based on information stated or implied in that passage. Circle the letter that appears before your choice.

Siberia (called Sibir in Russian) lies in Northern Asia. It is roughly divided into three areas: the central Siberian uplands (with high plateaus that extend from the Lena to the Yenisey rivers), the west Siberian lowlands (with both forests and grasslands that stretch from the Yenisey River to the Ural Mountains), and the east Siberian highlands (containing Mount Klyuchevskaya, Siberia's highest point).

While most Siberians now are white Russians, some descendants of the original Mongolian settlers remain in the area. The Mongolians have long been noted for their raising of livestock, including goats and reindeer.

1. The best title for this passage may be

   A. The People of Siberia   D. An Introduction to Siberia
   B. Siberian Agriculture   E. The Criminals of Russia
   C. Russians in Siberia

2. This passage most likely would be found in which of the following?

   A. A Russian history book   D. A travel brochure
   B. An encyclopedia   E. A sociology textbook
   C. A political treatise

3. According to the passage, which of the following is true of Mount Klyuchevskaya?

   A. It is in the capital city of Siberia.
   B. It is in the central Siberian highlands.
   C. It has the highest elevation of any place in Siberia.
   D. It is the highest mountain in Russia.
   E. All of the above.

4. Which of the following is a mountain range that may be found in Siberia?

   A. Klyuchevskaya   D. Ural
   B. Lena   E. None of the above
   C. Yenisey

   The image that many persons have of a scientist is of a gray-haired old man with a bushy white mustache bending over test tubes, or of a young, balding man with thick spectacles, peering through a microscope. Few people think of women scientists, yet some of the most important persons in science have been female.

   Dr. Florence Rena Sabin was elected to life membership in the New York Academy of Sciences, was a member of the Rockefeller Institute, and served as the president of the American Association of Anatomists. Dr. Sabin won recognition for her research work on tuberculosis, blood, and bone marrow, and was one of the first scientists to change the thrust of medicine from the cure of disease to the prevention of disease.

   Dr. Gladys Anderson Emerson was the first scientist to isolate Vitamin E from wheat germ oil and study its functions. With a Ph.D. in nutrition and biochemistry from the University of California at Berkeley (awarded in 1932), Dr. Emerson became a major contributor to information about the effect and uses of vitamins within the human body. Particularly interested in the relationship between diet and cancer, Dr. Emerson was appointed a research associate at the Sloan-Kettering Institute for Cancer Research in New York City.

A Nobel Prize was awarded in 1964 to Dr. Dorothy Crowfoot Hodgkin, Chancellor of Bristol University in England. Dr. Hodgkin was a crystallographer who was given the prize in recognition of her skill in using X-ray techniques to determine the structure of chemical compounds, particularly penicillin. Dr. Hodgkin's Nobel Prize for Chemistry was the third one given to a woman. Previous recipients were Marie Curie in 1911 and Irene Joliot-Curie (the daughter of Marie Curie) in 1935. Both previous recipients had shared the prize with their husbands; Dr. Hodgkin was the first woman to be recognized without the help of her spouse.

Dr. Lise Meitner, a nuclear physicist born in 1878, was responsible for the introduction of the term "nuclear fission." Dr. Meitner studied under Dr. Max Planck, originator of the quantum theory and winner of the Nobel Prize and became his assistant at the University of Berlin. She was also a friend of Neils Bohr, another Nobel Prize winner. It was to Neils Bohr that Dr. Meitner relayed her theories that the atom could be split to give off immense amounts of energy. Bohr took the news to America and helped begin the experiments that were eventually to lead to the development of the atomic bomb.

5. According to the passage, the first female recipient of the Nobel Prize for Chemistry was

A. Dr. Gladys Anderson Emerson
B. Dr. Lise Meitner
C. Marie Curie
D. Dr. Dorothy Crowfoot Hodgkin
E. Irene Joliot-Curie

6. Dr. Florence Rena Sabin is primarily remembered for her work with

   A. the prevention of disease
   B. Vitamin E and wheat germ oil
   C. atomic energy
   D. Niels Bohr
   E. cancer

7. The tone of this passage may best be described as

   A. sarcastic
   B. incredulous
   C. narrative
   D. whimsical
   E. critical

8. According to the passage, a crystallographer is

   A. one who grows crystals in a laboratory
   B. one who uses crystals in light and space experiments
   C. one who splits crystals into their smallest possible components
   D. one who charts the existence and frequency of crystals in nature
   E. the passage did not give a definition

Corporal punishment is a very emotional topic. Many persons firmly believe in the Biblical injunction "spare the rod and spoil the child," while others believe that those who are struck as children will grow up believing that violence is necessary to solve problems.

Only 50 years ago, children were regularly spanked in public schools and few persons protested. Now, if a child is spanked even for the most egregious violations, there may be lawsuits and criminal sanctions. Teachers and administrators must be very careful at all times to treat the persons of their charges with the same respect that they would show to adults. Striking a child even a mild blow in exasperation is forbidden by law in many cities and counties.

Teachers have difficulties at the other end of the spectrum as well. An instructor who hugs or strokes a child may be open to a charge of child abuse or sexual molestation. It is getting so bad that soon a teacher will not be able to touch or even talk to a child at all. Perhaps the time is right to introduce robots into the classroom.

9. The writer gives as an example of when a child might be struck as which of the following?

   A. when the child has not done his or her homework
   B. when the child has struck another child
   C. when the teacher is exasperated with the child
   D. when the teacher has been struck first by the child
   E. when the teacher has given several warnings to the child, all of which have been ignored

10. The writer mentions robots to make the point that

    A. soon teachers will be forced to function as unfeeling, uncaring robots
    B. soon students will be acting like robots
    C. robots are less likely to cause legal problems between teachers and parents
    D. robots are better teachers as they are less emotionally involved
    E. robots are more easily trained to instruct without digression

11. It can be inferred that the author feels

    A. teachers are too violent as a rule and should be watched very carefully
    B. children deserve regular discipline and must have it to do well in school
    C. teachers are too cowed by restrictions and too fearful of the consequences to be good, feeling teachers anymore
    D. the old ways of teaching were better
    E. all discipline should be left to the parents, not to the teachers

SENTENCE COMPLETION ANSWER KEY

1. A	3. C	5. A	7. C
2. B	4. D	6. B	

Explanations

1. **(A)** If a young man *runs* all the way across a room to be the first to ask a woman to dance, that woman must be very attractive. *Alluring* means charming, enticing, attractive. The other answers are all somewhat similar in meaning to one another. Puerile and jejune mean unsophisticated, immature, childish. No one would run across a room to ask such a woman to dance.

2. **(B)** The second part of the sentence tells you that the actor had *not* yet earned the right to be conceited. Since arrogant means conceited, you know that he had not yet earned the right to be arrogant either, and that his arrogance was unwarranted, improper, undeserved. Since he had not *yet* earned the right to be conceited, he must be somewhat of a beginner, new to the business. Note that in answer A the second word, "tyro," which means a beginner or a novice, would be correct, but the first word is wrong.

3. **(C)** One *admits* to something poorly done, such as admitting to a blunder. A blunder is a mistake, an error. The word "although" tells you that regardless of that error, Gabriella still thinks she has done well. To *maintain* is to state definitely, to reiterate. Note that while answers B and E have words that make sense in the first blank, the words for the second blank would be illogical when put into the sentence. If you chose either of those answers, you were tricked. Don't forget to read *both* words in the answer and insert them into the sentence.

4. **(D)** The words "after all" at the end of the sentence tell you that while the man *looks* mature, he is immature or callow. Therefore, his remarks must have belied, or shown to be untrue, his seeming maturity. Remarks that show one to be immature must be ridiculous, foolish, or inane. Note that while

answer B has a first word that could be correct, the second word is wrong.

5. **(A)** The key to this sentence is the word "surprised." You can deduce that the way Alan spoke of his ex-wife is the opposite of what she appeared to be to the speaker of the sentence. Therefore, the two blanks must have words that are somewhat opposite. Either he spoke well of her and she was unattractive, or he spoke ill of her and she was attractive. To speak disparagingly of someone is to speak ill of her, to criticize or belittle her. Note that answers B, C, and D are incorrect because they all have answers that follow logically from one another. For example, if one speaks glowingly of a woman, the listeners are not *surprised* to find that the woman is adorable. Answer E is somewhat humorous, but does not logically complete the sentence.

6. **(B)** The second half of the sentence says that one must have some virtues of one's own, meaning that one cannot simply copy the virtues of another. To *emulate* is to copy, to try to follow and be similar to.

7. **(C)** The key words are "route through the desert." You may infer that traveling through a desert is not the best way to go, and that a plan for doing so would not be practicable or feasible. Since such a route would not be feasible, the convicts would *postpone* their escape plans. Note that while the second word for answer A would be correct, the first word is wrong. To *implement* is to put into effect, to do.

READING COMPREHENSION ANSWER KEY

1. D	4. D	7. C	10. A
2. B	5. C	8. E	11. C
3. C	6. A	9. C	

Explanations

1. **(D)** The best title is one that summarizes the contents of the passage, but is neither too broad nor too specific. It gives a gen-

eral idea of what the passage is going to contain, what concepts are going to be discussed. Answers A, B, and C, while discussed in the passage, are each too specific to be a best title. Each is just one of several concepts covered. Answer E is not discussed at all.

2. **(B)** This passage gives a very brief overview of several factors about Siberia (such as its geography, people, and livestock). Such a brief summary would be found in an encyclopedia, where one goes to get an overall idea of a subject without going into a great many details. While history (in answer A) is briefly mentioned, this passage does not cover the history of the area sufficiently to be included in a history book. Answer C, a political treatise, is incorrect because the passage mentions nothing political at all. Answer D is incorrect because a travel brochure probably would give specific information on tourist sites and accommodations. Answer E is not even logical; little sociological discussion was given in the passage.

3. **(C)** This is a detail or specific fact question. In the last sentence of the first paragraph you are told that Mount Klyuchevskaya is Siberia's highest point. Note that for this type of question, you should go back to the passage to find the right answer. Do not trust yourself to remember the fact; reskim the passage to assure yourself of getting the answer correct.

4. **(D)** The Ural Mountains are mentioned in the first paragraph. Since the word "mountains" is given in the plural, you may infer that there is more than one mountain and that the Urals are a mountain range. Answers B and C are rivers, not mountain ranges. Answer A may have tricked you. Mount Klyuchevskaya is *a* mountain; you may not assume it is a mountain range.

5. **(C)** The fourth paragraph mentions that there were three women who had won the Nobel Prize for Chemistry. Dr. Hodgkin won it in 1964, Marie Curie won it in 1911, and Irene Joliot-Curie won it in 1935. From these facts, you know that the *first* woman to win it was Marie Curie. If you choose answer D, you either misread the question or relied on your memory, remembering that Dr. Hodgkin had been awarded the prize. For

a detail or specific fact question of this sort, *go back to the passage* and find the answer.

6. **(A)** Dr. Sabin is discussed in the second paragraph of the passage. There you are told that she was one of the first scientists to be concerned with the *prevention* of disease, rather than just its cure. Note that this is a rather tricky question because all of the answers given concern topics mentioned somewhere in the passage. Again, you should have taken the time to go back and find the specific answer in the passage. If you had written a brief note in the margin next to each paragraph telling *which* doctor that paragraph discussed, you would have been able to save time by finding the right paragraph immediately.

7. **(C)** The passage simply narrates information. There is no particular emotion involved. For a question of this sort, you do not go back to the passage. The answer will not be found there. You must infer the answer.

8. **(E)** The fourth paragraph tells you that Dr. Hodgkin was a crystallographer who won the Nobel Prize for Chemistry. However, it never defines the term "crystallographer." This type of question may be included to make you waste your time trying to find an answer. Go back and look, certainly, but if you cannot find a precise definition in just a few seconds, choose the answer that says the information was not given, and go on to the next question.

9. **(C)** The last sentence of the second paragraph states that a teacher may be forbidden by law to strike even a mild blow in exasperation. This is the only example given in the passage as a reason why the teacher might strike a child.

10. **(A)** This is the type of question where you had to think about your answer and ascribe a motive to the writer. You should *not* have gone back to the passage to look for an answer; one was not given there. Rarely will a passage directly state what an author's purpose is for writing a passage or making a specific statement. The author talks about robots after lamenting all the way through the passage that soon all human contact between students and teachers will be proscribed. You may

therefore assume that robots are introduced to make the point that soon teachers will be no more than robots themselves.

11. **(C)** This was a thinking question. You should *not* have gone back to the passage to look for a specific answer. This question is basically asking for "the moral of the story," the main point of the passage. The overriding theme of this passage is that there are so many restrictions and fears that teachers are handicapped in their efforts to be caring, feeling teachers. You may have been tricked by answer D. Just because the author makes the point that 50 years ago few people protested spanking children does not mean that he or she necessarily feels that the old ways of teaching were better. If you chose this answer, you read too much into a simple statement.

SCORE: NUMBER RIGHT:

NO PENALTY FOR WRONG ANSWERS

Hour Two: Math Review (Part I)

Set Your Clock. This hour's study is unusual in that no new question types are being introduced. Instead, you are going to learn basic mathematical concepts and rules which will be tested on the GRE. Of course, you cannot learn everything about mathematics, algebra, geometry, and other quantitative fields in just a two-hour period. Therefore, this section introduces you to those subjects that are tested repeatedly, and refreshes your memory on those concepts which you might have forgotten (such as certain units of measurement). Today you will concentrate on rules dealing with numbers, on units of measurement and on algebra. Tomorrow you will begin your study with geometry, fractions and decimals, and ratios.

How to Learn This Material

You probably will have learned the rules given in this section sometime during your high school or college days; however, you may have forgotten "exact" formulas or the precise way to set up an equation. The following steps will help you *memorize* such information so that you will have it fresh in your mind the day of the exam. Try the following steps to achieve the best results in the least time.

1. *Read all the information.* Before you try to begin memorizing the material, you should read *all* of it at least once. You may be surprised at how much material you retain even from one quick reading.

2. *Organize the information.* This means that you categorize the information given in terms of your personal knowledge of that material. In other words, try to distinguish those rules with which you are very familiar (perhaps you just finished a class in geometry, and you know all the geometric rules and formulas), from those rules which you once knew but are now uncertain of (such as algebra which you studied two years ago and haven't thought about since!). Once you have the material organized and cate-

gorized, you know which rules you may skim briefly, and which ones you should take the time to review very carefully.

3. *Make flash cards of the difficult concepts.* If you find that you are seeing material that is either new or very difficult for you, merely reading it will not be sufficient. Trying to memorize rules which are lost among many others on a printed page may be difficult as well. Try *rewriting the rules on flash cards.* Take index cards and write the rules and formulas on them. You may wish to make up your own supplementary examples to help you recall the rules.

4. *Have a friend test you.* Ask a friend to use the flash cards to test your knowledge. After you feel you have mastered the information on your cards, you may still have time to have that friend test you on the other, less difficult, concepts. The more you review this material, the quicker you will be able to determine which rule to use on the exam and the easier you will find it to solve the problem.

5. *Review the material when answering questions.* In coming study sessions, you will be learning about the three types of math questions you will encounter on the GRE. You will also be solving some practice problems. As you do each problem, stop and make a note of which formula or rule you used to solve that problem. Refer to these rules often to reinforce them in your mind.

The Rules

There are several basic concepts tested on the quantitative portion of the GRE. These concepts are introduced below, with critical formulas, rules, and vocabulary given.

Number Sets

Prime numbers: Prime numbers are integers which can be evenly divided only by themselves and 1. Examples: 2, 3, 5, 7, 11, 13, 17, 19, 23, 29.

Composite numbers: Composite numbers are the opposite of prime numbers. Composite numbers can be divided without a remainder by numbers other than themselves and 1. Examples: 4, 6, 8, 9, 12, 14, 15, 16, 18, 20.

NOTE: Do not confuse prime and composite numbers with odd and even numbers. While most prime numbers are odd (3, 5, 7, 9), one is even: 2. Composite numbers may be even (4, 6, 8) or odd (9, 15).

Whole numbers: A whole number is 0 or any positive multiple of 1. Whole numbers are usually defined as (0, 1, 2, 3 . . .) with the ". . ." meaning the set continues.

Integers: Integers are 0 and any positive (such as 2, 3) and negative (such as −2 or −3) whole numbers, as distinguished from fractions. Integers are usually defined as (. . . −3, −2, −1, 0, 1, 2, 3 . . .) with the ". . ." meaning the set continues in either direction.

- Integers include the set of whole numbers.

Rational numbers: Rational numbers are any numbers expressible as the quotient of two integers. Rational numbers are usually defined as a/b, where a and b are integers.

- Rational numbers include the sets of integers and whole numbers.

Irrational numbers: Irrational numbers are not capable of being expressed as the quotient of two integers. Irrational numbers are usually defined as $\neq a/b$.

- Irrational numbers do *not* include rational numbers, integers, or whole numbers. Pi (π) is an example of an irrational number.

Real numbers: Real numbers are all of the above terms, including whole numbers, integers, rational numbers, and irrational numbers.

Units of Measurement

LINEAR MEASUREMENTS

12 inches = 1 foot
36 inches = 1 yard
3 feet = 1 yard
5,280 feet = 1 mile
1,760 yards = 1 mile

- Metric units are *not* tested on the GRE. You are *not* required to be able to convert inches to centimeters, or yards to meters. If metric terms are used at all, they will be predefined for you.

AREA MEASUREMENTS

144 square inches = 1 square foot (12″ × 12″)
9 square feet = 1 square yard (3′ × 3′)

- You should not bother to memorize the square inches in a square yard, the square feet in a square mile, or the square yards in a square mile. Those numbers are too large to be tested; if they should appear, you may calculate them by squaring the linear measurements. For example, since there are 1,760 yards in a mile, there are (1,760 × 1,760) square yards in a square mile. It is highly unlikely this will be tested.

- NOTE: *All area measurements are in square units.*

VOLUME MEASUREMENTS

You may find volume measurements by cubing a number. For example, since there are 3 feet in a yard, there are (3′ × 3′ × 3′=) 27 cubic feet in a cubic yard. Do not bother memorizing all the cubic measurements; they may be calculated quickly if necessary.

LIQUID OR OTHER VOLUME MEASUREMENTS

2 cups = 1 pint
2 pints = 1 quart
2 quarts = 1 half gallon
2 half gallons = 1 gallon

16 cups = 1 gallon
8 pints = 1 gallon
4 quarts = 1 gallon
2 half gallons = 1 gallon

- NOTE AGAIN: You are not expected to be able to convert quarts to liters.

TIME MEASUREMENTS

60 seconds = 1 minute
60 minutes = 1 hour
24 hours = 1 day
7 days = 1 week
52 weeks = 1 year
365 days = 1 year
366 days = 1 leap year

MONTHS

January:	31 days
February:	28 days
(29 days in a leap year)	
March:	31 days
April:	30 days
May:	31 days
June:	30 days
July:	31 days
August:	31 days
September:	30 days
October:	31 days
November:	30 days
December:	31 days

- You may have learned the "Days Rhyme" in elementary school. It is useful in helping to remember how many days are in which months. It goes:

Thirty days has September,
April, June, and November.
All the rest have thirty-one
But Feb. has twenty-eight for fun!

Algebra

The word "algebra" is derived from the Arabic term "al-jabr," meaning the reunion of broken parts. Algebra is a mathematical system used to generalize mathematical operations by using variables. Variables are letters that represent values. Typical variables are X, Y, Z or A, B, C.

When you see an algebra problem, you are usually asked to find the value of the variable. The question might say, "Solve for X." To do so, you must get the variable, the X, on one side of the equation and everything else on the other side.

If your equation is $3X + 3 = 9X - 3$, the similar terms are the $3X$ and $9X$ and the $+3$ and the -3. To combine terms, you must get them on the same side of the equal sign. Move the -3 to the left. It now becomes $+3$, since any number moved from one side to the other changes its sign. (If it were $+$ before, it is now $-$. If it were $-$ before, it is now $+$.) Next, move the $3X$ to the right, making it $-3X$. Your equation is now $3 + 3 = 9X - 3X$ (If there is no $+$ or $-$ in front of a number, you assume it is positive.) *Combine* like terms. Add the $3 + 3$ to get 6. Subtract $9X - 3X$ to get $6X$. You now have $6 = 6X$.

The final step is to divide *both* sides by what is in front of the variable. You do this because you want to have the variable all by itself. Since a 6 is in front of the variable, divide both sides by a 6 to get

$$6/6 = 6X/6$$
$$1 = 1X; \ X = 1$$

Try another problem without the wordy explanation.

$$15 - 5X = 10X - 30$$
$$15 + 30 = 10X + 5X$$
$$45 = 15X$$
$$3 = X$$

This is the basic, simple type of algebra problem you will encounter. However, you may also have to multiply out variables such as

$$(a + b) (a + b).$$

You perform this multiplication one step at a time. Take the *a* in the first group and multiply it by the *a* in the second group to get a^2. Then take that same *a* in the first group and multiply it by the *b* in the second group to get *ab*.

Next, take the *b* in the first group and multiply it by the *a* in the second group to get *ba*. Take the *b* in the first group and multiply it by the *b* in the second group to get b^2.

You now have $a^2 + ab + ba + b^2$. The two central terms, *ab* and *ba*, are the same (when you multiply two numbers, you may do so in any order, such as 5×4 or 4×5). Combine terms to get $a^2 + 2ab + b^2$.

Try another problem without all the words:

$$(a - b) (a + b)$$
$$a \times a = a^2$$
$$a \times b = ab$$
$$-b \times a = -ab$$
$$-b \times b = -b^2$$
$$a^2 + ab - ab - b^2 = a^2 - b^2$$

(the $+ab$ and the $-ab$ cancel each other out).

While there are many other uses for algebra, if you have mastered these two concepts, you can do most of what you will find on the GRE. Again, you should be able to solve for a variable (find X) and multiply variables together $[(a+b)(a-b)]$.

3.

DAY THREE

Hour One: Math Review (Part II)

Set Your Clock. *Begin today's study by completing your math review—geometry, fractions and decimals, and ratios. In the second hour, you will meet the first of the GRE mathematics question styles: quantitative comparisons.*

Geometry

Closed Figures: Circles

The *midpoint* of a circle is a point in the center of the circle; the circle is usually named by its midpoint.

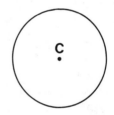

The *radius* of a circle is a line going from the midpoint of the circle to a point on the circumference of the circle.

The *diameter* of a circle is a straight line going from one side of a circle to the other, through the midpoint. A *diameter* is the same as two *radii*.

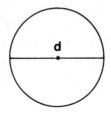

A *chord* is a line connecting *any* two points on a circle. The longest *chord* is the *diameter;* there are many other chords besides the *diameter.*

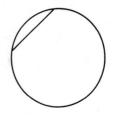

The *circumference* of a circle is its perimeter or outside line. The *circumference* is found using the formula $c = 2\pi r$ where r is the radius. Since $2r$ is the same as $1d$ (diameter), you may also use the formula $c = \pi d$. *Circumference* is always in linear units.

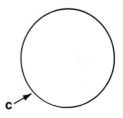

The interior angle measure of *any* circle is 360°.

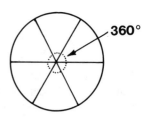

The *area* of a circle is found using the formula $A = \pi r^2$, where r is the radius. The *area* of a circle is always in square units.

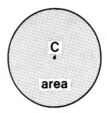

An *arc* is a part of a circle's circumference. You find it using the following
formula: Fraction (that the central
angle is of the total number of degrees
in the circle) times circumference. In
the example below, *XY* is the *arc*. The
central angle *XCY* measures 60°. The
total angle measure of a circle is 360°;
60° is 1/6 of 360°. Therefore, the *arc* is
1/6 of the circle's circumference. Find
the circumference ($C = 2\pi r$; here that
is 6π). $1/6 \times 6\pi = 1\pi$.

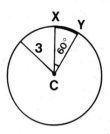

A *sector* is a part of a circle's area. You
find it using the following formula:
Fraction (that the central angle is of
the total number of degrees in the circle) times area. In the example below,
XCY is the *sector*. The central angle
XCY measures 120°. The total angle
measure of a circle is 360°; 120° is ⅓
of that. Therefore, the *sector* is ⅓ of the
circle's area. Find the area ($A = \pi r^2$;
here that is 36π). ⅓ $\times 36\pi = 12\pi$.

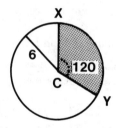

Closed Figures

Polygons are closed figures that lie in one plane. The name of a
polygon is determined by its number of sides and interior angles.

Triangle	3 sides/angles	Heptagon	7 sides/angles
Quadrilateral	4 sides/angles	Octagon	8 sides/angles
Pentagon	5 sides/angles	Nonagon	9 sides/angles
Hexagon	6 sides/angles	Decagon	10 sides/angles

The *exterior* angle measure of any polygon is 360°.

The *interior* angle measure of any polygon may be found using the following formula: $(S - 2)(180°)$ where S stands for the number of sides the figure has. When 2 is subtracted from the number of sides of a figure, the resulting number is the number of triangles into which the figure may be divided. Each triangle has an interior angle measure of 180°. Multiplying the number of triangles $(S - 2)$ by the interior angle measure of each triangle (180°) gives the interior angle measure of the whole polygon.

The *average* measure of one angle of a polygon may be found using the following formula: $\dfrac{(S - 2)(180°)}{S}$.

Find the total degrees in the interior of the figure; divide it by the number of angles. The number of interior angles is the same as the number of sides, S.

A *regular* polygon has *equal* sides and *equal* angles. Any angle in a regular polygon may be found using the formula $\dfrac{(S - 2)(180°)}{S}$ since all angles are equal.

Triangles are polygons with three sides. There are three types of triangles: *scalene* (with no equal sides and no equal angles); *isosceles* (with two equal sides and two equal angles); and *equilateral* (with three equal sides and three equal angles). An *equilateral* triangle is a *regular polygon* (since all of its sides and angles are equal).

Scalene

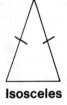

Isosceles

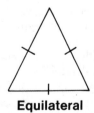

Equilateral

The interior angles of any triangle add up to 180°. The interior angles of any *quadrilateral* add up to 360° (since a quadrilateral may be divided into two triangles, as shown in the figure).

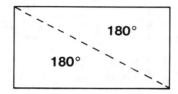

The area of a triangle is found using the formula: ½ *bh*, where *b* is the base and *h* is the height.

The area of a quadrilateral is found using the formula: *bh*, where *b* is the base and *h* is the height. NOTE: With some quadrilaterals, the letters change but the concept is the same. For example, the area of a rectangle is *lw*, where *l* is the length and *w* is the width. This is the same as *bh* because the base is the same as the length and the height is the same as the width. The area of a square is s^2, where *s* stands for side. This is the same as base times height as well, because all sides of a square are equal.

The area of a *trapezoid* is $\frac{1}{2}(b_1 + b_2)h$ where b_1 stands for one base, b_2 stands for the other, and *h* stands for the height. Since in a *trapezoid*, opposite bases are parallel but not necessarily equal, the average length of the bases must be found.

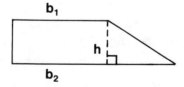

Simple Angles

An angle measuring less than 90° is called *acute*.

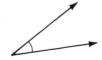

An angle measuring exactly 90° is called *right*. It is often indicated by a small box in the angle.

An angle measuring more than 90° but less than 180° is called *obtuse*.

An angle measuring exactly 180° is called *straight*. Angles along a straight line must add up to 180°.

An angle measuring more than 180° but less than 360° is called *reflexive*.

Angles that add up to 90° are called *complementary*.

Angles that add up to 180° are called *supplementary*.

Angles that are opposite one another are called *vertical* angles. Vertical angles are equal.

Around two parallel lines crossed by a transversal, all acute angles are equal and all obtuse angles are equal. (If you have difficulty determining which angles are acute and which are obtuse, you might note that all angles *in the same position* are equal. Angles 1 and 5 in the figure are both in the upper left corner and are equal.)

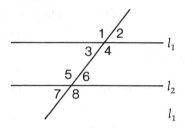

Fractions and Decimals

All fractions may be converted to decimals and percentages. You should *memorize* the following most common fractions for use on the exam.

$\frac{1}{2}$ = .50 = 50%	$\frac{1}{6} \sim$ .16 = 16⅔%	$\frac{1}{8}$ = .125 = 12.5%
$\frac{1}{3} \sim$ .33 = 33⅓%	$\frac{5}{6} \sim$ .83 = 83⅓%	$\frac{3}{8}$ = .375 = 37.5%
$\frac{2}{3} \sim$ .66 = 66⅔%	$\frac{1}{7} \sim$ .14 $\sim$ 14%	$\frac{5}{8}$ = .625 = 62.5%
$\frac{1}{4}$ = .25 = 25%	$\frac{2}{7} \sim$ .29 $\sim$ 29%	$\frac{7}{8}$ = .875 = 87.5%
$\frac{3}{4}$ = .75 = 75%	$\frac{3}{7} \sim$ .43 $\sim$ 43%	$\frac{1}{9} \sim$ .11 $\sim$ 11%
$\frac{1}{5}$ = .20 = 20%	$\frac{4}{7} \sim$ .57 $\sim$ 57%	$\frac{2}{9} \sim$ .22 $\sim$ 22%
$\frac{2}{5}$ = .40 = 40%	$\frac{5}{7} \sim$ .71 $\sim$ 71%	$\frac{4}{9} \sim$ .44 $\sim$ 44%
$\frac{3}{5}$ = .60 = 60%	$\frac{6}{7} \sim$ .86 $\sim$ 86%	$\frac{5}{9} \sim$ .56 $\sim$ 56%
$\frac{4}{5}$ = .80 = 80%		$\frac{7}{9} \sim$ .78 $\sim$ 78%
		$\frac{8}{9} \sim$ .89 $\sim$ 89%

If you forget a fraction/decimal equivalency, you may find it mathematically by dividing the bottom number into the top.

Fractions and decimals become *larger* when *added* but *smaller* when *multiplied*. $\frac{1}{3} + \frac{1}{3} = \frac{2}{3}$, $\frac{1}{3} \times \frac{1}{3} = \frac{1}{9}$

Fractions and decimals become *smaller* when subtracted but *larger* when *divided*. $\frac{2}{3} - \frac{1}{3} = \frac{1}{3}$, $\frac{2}{3} \div \frac{1}{3} = \left(\dfrac{\frac{2}{3}}{\frac{1}{3}} \cdot \dfrac{\frac{3}{1}}{\frac{3}{1}} = \dfrac{\frac{6}{3}}{1} = \right)$ 2.

A decimal may be converted to a percent by moving the decimal point two places to the right. .625 = 62.5%.

A fraction is a part divided by a whole. The formula is sometimes expressed as *is/of*, as in the following example: What fraction *of* 50 is 25? $\frac{25}{50} = \frac{1}{2}$.

Ratios

A *ratio* may be found using the formula *of/to*. Example: What is the ratio *of* 8 dogs *to* 2 cats? 8/2 = 4/1 or 4:1.

To use a ratio to find a *total*, *add* the numbers in the ratio. The total must be a *multiple* of that sum. Example: With a ratio of 8 dogs to 2 cats, the total must be (8 + 2 = 10) a multiple of 10. There may be 10, 20, 30, 40, etc., dogs and cats. There could not be 11, 22, 33, etc.

To use a ratio and a partial total to find a specific number, look for the *number of sets*. Example: If there is a ratio of 8 dogs to 2 cats, and there are 16 dogs, how many cats are there? Since 16 is *two sets* of 8, there must also be *two sets* of 2, or 4 cats. If there is a ratio of 6 dogs to 7 cats, and there are 35 cats, how many dogs are there? Since 35 is *five sets* of 7, there must also be *five sets* of 6, or 30 dogs.

Around two parallel lines crossed by a transversal, all acute angles are equal and all obtuse angles are equal. (If you have difficulty determining which angles are acute and which are obtuse, you might note that all angles *in the same position* are equal. Angles 1 and 5 in the figure are both in the upper left corner and are equal.)

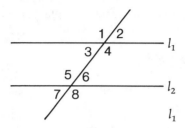

Fractions and Decimals

All fractions may be converted to decimals and percentages. You should *memorize* the following most common fractions for use on the exam.

½ = .50 = 50%	⅙ ~ .16 = 16⅔%	⅛ = .125 = 12.5%
⅓ ~ .33 = 33⅓%	⅚ ~ .83 = 83⅓%	⅜ = .375 = 37.5%
⅔ ~ .66 = 66⅔%	⅐ ~ .14 ~ 14%	⅝ = .625 = 62.5%
¼ = .25 = 25%	2/7 ~ .29 ~ 29%	⅞ = .875 = 87.5%
¾ = .75 = 75%	3/7 ~ .43 ~ 43%	⅑ ~ .11 ~ 11%
⅕ = .20 = 20%	4/7 ~ .57 ~ 57%	2/9 ~ .22 ~ 22%
⅖ = .40 = 40%	5/7 ~ .71 ~ 71%	4/9 ~ .44 ~ 44%
⅗ = .60 = 60%	6/7 ~ .86 ~ 86%	5/9 ~ .56 ~ 56%
⅘ = .80 = 80%		7/9 ~ .78 ~ 78%
		8/9 ~ .89 ~ 89%

If you forget a fraction/decimal equivalency, you may find it mathematically by dividing the bottom number into the top.

Fractions and decimals become *larger* when *added* but *smaller* when *multiplied*. ⅓ + ⅓ = ⅔, ⅓ × ⅓ = ⅑

Fractions and decimals become *smaller* when subtracted but *larger* when *divided*. $\frac{2}{3} - \frac{1}{3} = \frac{1}{3}$, $\frac{2}{3} \div \frac{1}{3} = \left(\dfrac{\frac{2}{3}}{\frac{1}{3}} \cdot \dfrac{\frac{3}{1}}{\frac{3}{1}} = \dfrac{\frac{6}{3}}{1} = \right)$ 2.

A decimal may be converted to a percent by moving the decimal point two places to the right. .625 = 62.5%.

A fraction is a part divided by a whole. The formula is sometimes expressed as *is/of*, as in the following example: What fraction *of* 50 is 25? $\frac{25}{50} = \frac{1}{2}$.

Ratios

A *ratio* may be found using the formula *of/to*. Example: What is the ratio *of* 8 dogs *to* 2 cats? 8/2 = 4/1 or 4:1.

To use a ratio to find a *total, add* the numbers in the ratio. The total must be a *multiple* of that sum. Example: With a ratio of 8 dogs to 2 cats, the total must be (8 + 2 = 10) a multiple of 10. There may be 10, 20, 30, 40, etc., dogs and cats. There could not be 11, 22, 33, etc.

To use a ratio and a partial total to find a specific number, look for the *number of sets*. Example: If there is a ratio of 8 dogs to 2 cats, and there are 16 dogs, how many cats are there? Since 16 is *two sets* of 8, there must also be *two sets* of 2, or 4 cats. If there is a ratio of 6 dogs to 7 cats, and there are 35 cats, how many dogs are there? Since 35 is *five sets* of 7, there must also be *five sets* of 6, or 30 dogs.

Hour Two: Quantitative Comparisons

Set Your Clock. You will have a full hour to review the first of three types of mathematics questions you will find on the GRE. Quantitative Comparisons are quite different from most math questions you have had on standardized exams or school tests over the years. Please take the time, therefore, to go through this section especially carefully. Because the questions in this section are so unusual, you want to make certain that you understand their format precisely before going on to the actual exam.

What You Will See

The mathematics sections of the GRE generally have 30 questions. Fifteen of these are quantitative comparisons; the remaining 15 are problem solving, including data interpretation. Generally, quantitative comparisons are the first 15 questions.

Question Style

Each quantitative comparison consists of information given in two columns. At the top of the page will be the titles Column A and Column B. Information will be printed in both columns for each question. Such information may be a phrase, a word, numerals, or symbols.

EXAMPLE:

COLUMN A	COLUMN B
The cost of 10 cars at $8,000 each	The cost of 8 cars at $10,000 each

EXAMPLE:

$\sqrt{36}$	6^2

If information is to be used in both columns, that information is centered between the two columns.

EXAMPLE: $X < 0$

X^2 X^3

A variable (a letter such as X or Y or A or B) or a symbol (such as # or *) represents the same number or operation throughout the problem.

EXAMPLE: $(X + 4)^2 - 3$ $(X - 3)^2 - 4$

NOTE: Do not solve for X in one problem and then assume that X retains that value into the next question. For example, in one question, X may equal 3, while in the next question X may equal 1/5 and in the third question may equal 0.

Any diagrams or figures will *not necessarily* be drawn to scale. This means that you are not able simply to look at a problem and use your eyes to determine angle measurements or sizes. For example, in the figure below, you cannot automatically assume that angle X is larger than angle Y.

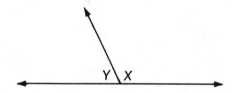

Summary. Your problems are not actually "questions" in the strictest sense of the word. Rarely will you see a complete statement, such as "What is the value of X?" Instead, you will simply see "X."

The Answer Choices

This unusual question type has *four* possible answers. *Note that this is the only portion of the exam where there are only four possible answers rather than five.* You have answer choices A, B, C, and D, as opposed to your standard choices A, B, C, D, and E. If you guess an answer, never fill in an E; you will of course have no chance of guessing the correct answer by doing so.

Quantitative comparisons require you to compare quantities. You will see two quantities, one in Column A and one in Column B. You are to compare them and determine whether one is larger, whether they are equal, or whether you cannot make the comparison.

If the quantity in Column A is larger than the quantity in Column B, your answer is A.

EXAMPLE: COLUMN A   COLUMN B

            ⅙   16%

In this example, the quantity in Column A is larger than the quantity in Column B. You might have been tempted to say they are equal, but 1/6 is actually 16.$\overline{66}$%, a number slightly larger than 16%. This type of question is common. It takes only a second to answer, but you have to be very careful not to be too complacent, to fall into the trap of automatically assuming that two similar-appearing quantities are exactly equal.

If the quantity in Column B is larger than the quantity in Column A, your answer is B.

EXAMPLE: COLUMN A   COLUMN B

            33%   ⅓

In this example, the quantity in Column B is larger than the quantity in Column A. The fraction ⅓ is actually 33 ⅓%, which is larger than 33%. Again, this is a simple, quickly answered question—if you are careful.

If the quantity in Column A is equal to the quantity in Column B, your answer is C.

EXAMPLE: COLUMN A   COLUMN B

            ⅗   60%

Because 3/5 is *exactly* equal to 60%, the quantities are equal. If, for some reason, you have not memorized all of the fraction/percentage equivalencies, you could quickly solve this problem by dividing 3 by 5. Your answer is exactly .6, which is the same as 60%.

If you *cannot* make a comparison between the quantities in the two columns, your answer is D.

EXAMPLE: COLUMN A   COLUMN B

The number of   30
days in a month

You do not have enough information to compare the quantities. To find the number in Column A, you have to know *which* month you are considering: February (with 28, or even 29 in a leap year), March with 31, or April with 30? Without the information, you cannot compare the quantities. NOTE: Even if Column A had been 30 and Column B had had the statement, the answer would still be D. It makes no difference whether you cannot find an answer for Column A, for Column B, or for both columns.

Review

A = Column A is larger
B = Column B is larger
C = Both columns are equal
D = The columns can't be compared

Directions

The math section is preceded by rather lengthy directions. If you see and understand them now, you will not need to spend time reading and trying to comprehend them when you take the actual exam.

The directions begin by stating that "all numbers used are real numbers." You learned in yesterday's lesson that the set of real numbers includes all whole numbers, integers, rational numbers, and irrational numbers. In general, the set of real numbers includes everything you have ever worked with. There are numbers called imaginary numbers; they are much too sophisticated to be tested on this exam. Don't be concerned, therefore, with this direction.

The second direction is a set of statements regarding any figures drawn on the exam. Let's go through each of these in detail.

First, you are told that you may assume as correct the positions of points, angles, and regions. This means that if on a number line, X is to the right of Y, X is larger than Y.

EXAMPLE:

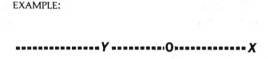

Here, Y is negative (since it is to the left of 0) and X is positive (since it is to the right of 0). Any positive number is greater than any negative number.

Second, you are told that angle measures are positive. This means that there are no angles that measure 0° or negative numbers, such as −60° or −90°.

Third, you are told that "you may assume that lines that appear to be straight are straight." This simply means that no one is trying to trick you with lines that are slightly bent or curved.

Fourth, you are told that "unless otherwise indicated, figures lie in a plane." This statement is for those persons who have had a lot of upper level geometry. It simply means that standard, beginning geometry is all you need to know to do any problems on this exam.

Finally, you are told that "unless you are told a figure is drawn to scale, you may not assume it is so." This is similar to what you heard before. In other words, you cannot trust your eyes to tell you that one angle is larger than another, or that a particular angle is a right (90°) angle.

After you go through all the directions on the figures, you are given your "standard directions." These tell you that you will see two quantities which are to be compared, and that you should choose A if the quantity in Column A is larger, B if the quantity in Column B is larger, C if both quantities are equal, and D if you cannot compare the quantities. These answer choices were discussed in greater detail earlier in this material.

After the directions is a brief note reminding you never to choose E. *Please remember this:* If you find that you have only one minute left, but you have several problems incomplete, you *do* want to fill in some ovals to take a chance on getting some answers correct. However, be certain not to fill in oval E and waste your guess.

Lastly, you are told that common information (information to be used in one or both of the columns) is centered between the columns.

An example will be given at the end of these directions. It is generally a very, very simplistic one, such as the difference between adding 1 to 1 and subtracting 1 from 1.

Summary. The directions take up about ¾ of a column and can look very intimidating. If you understand the brief analysis given above, you can skim them or skip them entirely and go right to the problems.

How to Do the Problems

Since you are only comparing quantities, not looking for a final, precise answer, you want to avoid doing any more calculating than absolutely necessary. The following steps will help you make the best use of your time.

1. *Read both columns.* Take the time to read any information centered between the columns, then read Column A *and* Column B. Do *not* fall into the trap of beginning to calculate an answer for Column A before you read Column B. Chances are you will not have to do any calculations at all.

EXAMPLE:	COLUMN A	COLUMN B
	356×234	$65 \times 0 \times 1,281$

Had you read only Column A, you might have wasted your time actually multiplying out these numbers. However, had you done the smart thing and looked at Column B, you would have noted that one of the numbers to be multiplied is a 0. Since *any number or numbers* multiplied by a 0 must equal 0, you automatically know that Column B is 0. Since both numbers in Column A are positive, you know that the product of those numbers must be positive. *Any* positive number is greater than 0; therefore, *regardless of the actual value* in Column A, Column A is greater than Column B. Choose answer A.

2. *Look at your operations.* Operations are what you do to the numbers, such as addition, subtraction, multiplication, and division. Often you will find that the operation makes a difference in the answer, so that you don't have to work out the entire problem.

EXAMPLE: COLUMN A   COLUMN B

               $\frac{1}{2} + \frac{1}{4}$ $\frac{1}{2} \times \frac{1}{4}$

When you add fractions, they become *larger*. When you multiply fractions, they become *smaller*. Since the fractions are the same in both columns, and Column A becomes larger while Column B becomes smaller, you know that Column B must be smaller than Column A. Choose answer A.

3. *Look for equal proportions.* You may find that the two columns are saying the same thing in two different ways. For example, multiplication is commutative, which means that it may be done in any order. $5 \times 4 = 4 \times 5$. If Column A said 456×890 and Column B said 890×456, you would know to choose answer C since both columns have equal quantities being multiplied. Often this same principle is tested in a slightly more sophisticated way.

EXAMPLE: COLUMN A   COLUMN B

               300% of   200% of 75
               200% of
               25

In Column A, 300% of 200% is the same as 3 times and 2 times, or 6 times 25. In Column B, 200% is the same as 2 times. Since 25 is ⅓ of 75, and you are multiplying it 3 times as often as you are multiplying 75, the columns are equal (6 × 25 = 150; 2 × 75 = 150). Choose answer C.

4. *Solve the problem.* If all else fails and you cannot find any short cuts or tricks, go ahead and work the problem through. Usually there will be some short cut; however, don't spend so much time looking for it that you defeat your own purpose. If you do work through the problem, try to stop as soon as possible. In other words, don't do each and every calculation out to its final steps. If you see that Column A is going to have 65 × 48 while Column B is going to have 68 × 49, you know that Column B is going to be larger (since each number to be multiplied in Column B is larger than each number to be multiplied in Column A).

EXAMPLE   COLUMN A   COLUMN B

−465 × 36   21 × −797

In this instance, there are no obvious short cuts. Each column has one negative and one positive. Each column uses multiplication; therefore, each answer will be negative. When you multiply Column A out, you get −16,740. Column B's product is −16,737. As you see, the answers are so close that estimation would be difficult.

NOTE: When you do notice that you have to work out a problem of this sort, decide whether doing so is worth your time. You may find that you can go through five or six other problems using short cuts in the time it would take you to work all the way through this one problem.

Traps to Avoid

When *reading* the quantitative comparison questions, you should be careful to avoid the following traps:

1. *Do not carry over information from one problem to another.* If you just found out that "X = 15" in one problem don't assume that it

has the same value in another problem. It is very easy to do so; watch yourself carefully.

2. *Don't misread the operation signs.* Many problems have been missed because a student saw that the numbers in Column A were separated by plus signs and just automatically assumed that the numbers in Column B were as well. Perhaps Column A called for addition while Column B called for subtraction. Look at the signs in *both* columns.

3. *Don't gloss over the additional information that is centered between the columns.* Often such information gives *vital* facts, such as whether a number is positive ($X>0$) or negative ($X<0$).

When *solving* the quantitative comparison questions, you should be careful to avoid the following traps.

1. *Don't make rough estimates unless you know that the quantities are so far apart that doing so is expected.* In other words, with a problem like the one given earlier (where Column A came out to be $-16,740$ and Column B came out to be $-16,737$), making an estimate would possibly cause you to miss the problem. Look carefully before you estimate.

2. *Keep your calculations neat.* This may sound elementary, but doing sloppy calculations has led to many a missed problem. If you don't keep track of your positive and negative signs and make certain your decimal point is properly positioned, you could easily miss a question that should be very basic.

3. *Do not choose answer E under any circumstances.*

Time-saving Suggestions

1. *Estimate whenever feasible.* Often, you will find that you can make a very rough estimate, or simply determine that one column will be positive while the other will be negative or zero. Don't do any specific calculations unless absolutely necessary.

2. *Skip around within the section.* As long as you keep track of your numbering, you should feel free to skip problems you find trou-

blesome. If you don't understand a problem, or have no idea how to begin working it, choose any answer at random and fill in your answer grid. Place an arrow next to the problem in your test booklet (don't make stray marks on your answer grid) so that you can go back to it if you have a chance. If you understand a problem only too well, and know that you could do it but it would take you some time for lengthy calculations, you may also wish to skip the problem and return to it later.

3. *Use the information given.* Often, one column (usually Column B) will have a specific number. Work backwards, using it to help you with Column A. For example, if Column A is 5026/13 and Column B is 386, just multiply 386 by 13 and see what you get. You will get, in this instance, 5018, telling you that 5026/13 must be larger than 386. If you worked the problem all the way through, you would find that 5026/13 = 386.61538. Most people find that multiplying numbers is easier than dividing them. Use the numbers given and work with them.

Practice Exam: Quantitative Comparisons

Please take the following practice exam on quantitative comparisons. The quantitative ability section of the actual GRE has 30 questions; generally the first 15 of those are quantitative comparisons. This practice exam consists of 15 questions with an answer key and explanatory answers following. (The second type of math problems, problem solving, will be tested in the next exam.) Score yourself, giving yourself one point for each correct answer. Do *not* subtract points for wrong answers.

NOTE: On the actual exam, you are likely to see as many as four examples following the directions, preceding the problems. In the interests of time and space, only one example is given here.

Quantitative Comparisons

General Information

All numbers used are real numbers.
You may assume as correct the positions of points, angles, and regions.
Angle measures are positive.
You may assume that lines that appear to be straight are straight.
Unless otherwise indicated, figures lie in a plane.
Unless you are told a figure is drawn to scale, you may not assume it is so.

DIRECTIONS: Compare the quantity in Column A with the quantity in Column B and choose answer

A if the quantity in Column A is larger
B if the quantity in Column B is larger
C if both quantities are equal
D if you cannot determine the relationship between the quantities

Write in your answer choice next to each question number.
There is no answer choice E.
Information regarding one or both of the quantities is given centered between the columns.

	COLUMN A	COLUMN B
1.	Average of 5, 7, 9, 11, 13	Average of 7, 8, 9, 10, 11
2.	Area of a circle whose longest chord is 4	Area of a circle of radius 2

3. $$3Y = 6X$$

| X | 1 |

4.

| Area of AEC | 50% of the area of $ABCD$ |

5. $$\text{Set } Z = (2, 3, 4, 5, 6, 7)$$

| Number of prime numbers in Set Z | Number of composite numbers in Set Z |

6. $$X^2 = Y$$

| X | Y |

7.

| The dress sold for 125% of its original cost | |
| Profit | $25.00 |

8.

| The average weight of three men is 150 lb. | |
| Total weight of the men | 400 lb |

9.

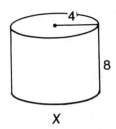

X

Volume of cylinder X	160π cubic units

10.

The ratio of men to women is 9:4

Number of people	13

11.

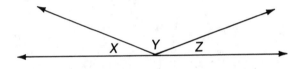

Supplement to angle X	Supplement to angle Y

12.

Number of pints required to fill a 40-gallon pool	Number of ounces in 20 lb

13.

$$18X - 12 = 6X + 24$$

X	6

14.

a, *b* are positive

$(a - b)^2$	$(a + b)^2$

15.

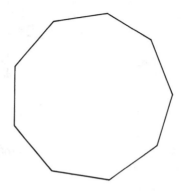

| Number of degrees in interior angles of the figure | 1300 |

ANSWER KEY

1. C	5. A	9. B	13. B
2. C	6. D	10. D	14. B
3. D	7. D	11. D	15. B
4. C	8. A	12. C	

Explanations

1. **(C)** You *could* have wasted time doing this averaging problem "the old-fashioned way," adding all the numbers and dividing by the number of numbers. However, you should have noted that in Column A the numbers are evenly spaced (they are two units apart) such that the number in the middle is automatically the average: 9. In Column B, the numbers are consecutive (they come right after one another), such that the number in the middle is automatically the average: 9. Note that this type of problem should only have taken you a few seconds; the columns are equal. Choose answer C.

2. **(C)** In Column A, you have to know that the longest chord in a circle *is* the diameter. Therefore, Column A is really asking you what the area of a circle of diameter 4 is. Since the diame-

ter is the same as two radii, you know that the radius of that circle is 2. *Do not bother finding the actual area.* Had you read *both* columns before doing any work, you would recognize that Column B asks for exactly the same thing: the area of a circle of radius 2. While finding the area with such a simple radius would not be difficult, you need not take even the few seconds required. Choose answer C.

3. **(D)** This question might have tricked you. If you put answer C, you were careless. Because $3Y = 6X$, it takes twice as many Xs to reach a quantity as it takes Ys. For example, if Y were 2, X would have to be 1. If Y were 4, X would be 2. However, you know only the proportion or ratio of Y to X. You don't know any exact numbers. X could be 1, in which case Y would be 2. Or X could be greater than 1 or less than 1. (Both X and Y could be 0.) You have insufficient information to solve for an actual value for X. Choose answer D.

4. **(C)** AEC is a triangle inscribed in the rectangle ABCD. Any triangle inscribed in a rectangle must have an area ½ that of the rectangle. The area of a triangle is ½ *bh*, one-half base times height. Here, the base is AC and the height is FE. (FE must be equal to AB and CD because it is parallel to those lines.) For the rectangle ABCD, the area is *lw*, length times width. The length is CD and the width is AC. Therefore, you are using the same values to find the area of the rectangle as to find the area of the triangle. Since the triangle multiplies the values by ½, its area must be ½ that of the rectangle. Choose answer C.

5. **(A)** Prime numbers are those which may be evenly divided only by themselves and 1. The prime numbers in Set Z are 2, 3, 5, 7; there are four. Composite numbers are the opposite of prime numbers (any number that is not prime is composite). Composite numbers may be divided evenly by numbers other than just themselves and 1. The composite numbers in Set Z are 4 and 6; there are two. *Note the trap.* If you forgot that 2 is prime (it is, in fact, the only even prime), you might have chosen answer C, believing that there are three primes and three composites. Since 2 is prime, there are more primes than composites. Choose answer A.

6. **(D)** This was another difficult, tricky question. You might have automatically (and carelessly) thought that Y must be larger than X, because X had to be multiplied by itself to become as large as Y. However, don't forget that both numbers could be 0 or 1. This means that the variables *could* be equal or (if you used other values, such as 3 and 9), X could be smaller than Y. Since you could have two different situations, you cannot determine the relationship between the quantities. Choose answer D.

7. **(D)** The formula to be used in this type of problem is $S = C + P$, Sales price equals Cost plus Profit. In order to find out one specific number, you need at least one number to begin with. Here, you are given no specific number, just a percentage. You know that the profit was 25% of the original cost; however, you have no idea of the original cost. Therefore, you cannot assume that the original cost was $100, so that 25% of it would be $25. If the original cost were only $40, the profit would be a mere $10. If the original cost were $400, the profit would be $100. Without more information, you cannot determine the relationship between the columns. Choose answer D.

8. **(A)** If three men averaged 150 lb each, their total weight must be 3 times that average, or $(150 \times 3 =)$ 450 lb. It makes no difference that you don't know exactly how much each man weighed; you are only asked to find the total weight. Even if one man weighed 100 lb, a second weighed 200 lb, and a third weighed 150 lb, the total is the same. If you chose answer D, assuming that you didn't have enough information to answer this question, you didn't think the question through. Since the three men total 450 lb, choose answer A.

9. **(B)** The volume of a figure is found by multiplying the area of the base times the height. With a cylinder, the base is a circle. The area of a circle is πr^2. Here, r is 4, so that $\pi r^2 = 16\pi$. Next, you would multiply 16 π by 8. However, you should not actually do this multiplication. When you look at Column B and see 160, you should know that it is the larger number. You know that 16 times 10 would be 160; here you are multiplying

16 by a mere 8. Thus, your answer must be less than 160 and Column B must be larger. Choose answer B.

10. **(D)** Did this question trick you? If the ratio of men to women is 9:4, there are 9 men for every 4 women. Therefore, there could be a total of 13 people, 9 men and 4 women. Or, there could be 26 people, 18 men and 8 women. Or there could be 39 people, 27 men and 12 women. In other words, there could be any number of people, as long as the ratio of men to women remains 9:4. This means that there must be a total number of people that is a multiple of 13. There could not be, for example, 14 people, because there would be 9 men, 4 women—and one something or other left over! The total must always be a multiple of the sum of the numbers in the ratio, but it could be any multiple. Choose answer D.

11. **(D)** Angles X, Y, and Z are all along a straight line and thus are supplementary. Angles that are supplementary add up to 180°. The supplement to angle X is the sum of angles Y and Z. The supplement to angle Y is the sum of angles X and Z. Since Z remains constant, you are really comparing X to Y. Since you cannot assume the figure is drawn to scale, you cannot assume angles X and Y are equal. You don't have enough information to compare the quantities. Choose answer D.

12. **(C)** If you know your units of measurement (which you should have memorized), this is a simple problem. You should *not* have done any calculations at all. Since there are 8 pints to a gallon, there would be 8 × 40 pints in a 40-gallon pool. Since there are 16 ounces in a pound, there would be 16 × 20 ounces in 20 lb. Note the proportional relationship between the columns: 8 is ½ of 16; 40 is twice 20. Therefore, regardless of what the actual result is, the columns are equal. Try to look for these types of short cuts whenever possible. Choose answer C.

13. **(B)** This is a standard algebra problem. You must move the numbers to have all the X terms on one side and all the non-X terms on the other. Move the 6X to the left, making it −6X. Remember that when you move from one side of the equals

sign to the other, you make a (+) into a (−) and a (−) into a (+). Move the −12 from the left to the right, making it +12. Now you have $18X - 6X = 24 + 12$. Combine like terms to get $12X = 36$. Divide both sides through by the 12 (so that you end up with just X on one side) to get $36/12 = 3$. $X = 3$. Choose answer B.

14. **(B)** The key to this problem is the information that a and b are *positive*. This means that they are not negative and they are not zero. In this case, adding a positive to a must make the quantity larger than subtracting that same number. NOTE: This problem was a commonsense one; you should not have bothered to write out all the terms. However, if you did not see the "point" of the question, you could have used another short cut.

You should have *memorized* the fact that $(a - b)^2 = a^2 - 2ab + b^2$ and the fact that $(a + b) = a^2 + 2ab + b^2$. The a^2's and the b^2's are the same in both columns; only the $-2ab$ and the $+2ab$ are different. Since a and b are positive, you know that a $+2ab$ must be larger than a $-2ab$. Choose answer B.

15. **(B)** The figure is a nonagon (it has nine sides). To find the total interior degree measure, subtract 2 from the number of sides and multiply by 180°. You should remember the formula $(S - 2)(180°)$ where S represents the number of sides. By subtracting 2 from the number of sides, you find the number of triangles. Since each triangle contains 180°, multiply the number of triangles by 180°. Here, you have $7 \times 180°$. Unfortunately, the numbers are too close to estimate in this instance; you should (for a change) do the calculations. Seven times 180° = 1260°. Choose answer B.

SCORE: NUMBER RIGHT:

NO PENALTY FOR WRONG ANSWERS

4.

DAY FOUR

Hour One: Problem Solving

Set Your Clock. This hour will be devoted to the second type of mathematics question you will find on the GRE, the problem-solving question. You will be glad to know that this type of question is much more familiar, and consequently much easier to understand, than the quantitative comparison question. Some of the problem-solving questions, however, are based on data presented in charts, graphs and tables. Many test-takers are intimidated by such questions. You will spend your second hour of study today learning about data interpretation questions.

The Question Style

The problem-solving question is the basic multiple-choice mathematics question you have seen on standardized exams before. You are given a question to answer or a problem to solve. You will then be given five answer choices; you are to choose the correct one. There will be only one correct answer. Occasionally, a question asks you to find an approximate solution. In such an instance, choose the best answer, the one that is closest to the precise answer.

Most problem-solving questions will be relatively short. Some will have additional information, in the form of a chart, graph, table, or figure, in the margin or above the problem. Some charts, graphs, tables, or figures are used in more than one problem. If that is the case, there will be a note stating "Questions —— through —— refer to the following figure."

Finding the Answer

To answer a problem-solving question, you should take the following approach:

Step One: *Read the entire question very carefully.* You may even wish to circle or underline some important information. If the problem is very long (such as a word problem), such notation can be quite helpful.

Step Two: *Determine exactly what the question is asking.* Do you have to find a percentage, a ratio, a total, or a fraction? Do you have to find a final solution or merely an intermediate step? Are you asked to find A's age or B's age? Be very careful to answer what the question is asking. Often the answer key will have specially written "trap" answers, answers that you might choose if you didn't read the question carefully.

Step Three: *Predict what you need to do to find the answer.* Note that this is different from actually doing the steps. Here, you want to determine how many calculations you have to make, how much time this problem is going to take, how hard it is going to be to solve. If you find that the problem is very hard, requiring skills you are weak in, you may want to postpone doing it until the end of the section. If you find that the problem is very simple, but will require several time-consuming steps, you will have to decide whether or not it is worth spending that much time on one problem.

Step Four: *Predict an answer form.* An answer form is not the answer itself; it is the form in which the answer will be given. For example, if you are asked to find the area of a figure, the form of the answer will be in square units. If you are asked to find the volume of a figure, the form of the answer will be in cubic units.

Step Five: *Look at the answer choices.* This step is critical. If you look at the answer choices, you can probably eliminate two or three answers immediately because they are in the wrong form (square units instead of cubic units, a fraction instead of a percentage). Looking at the answer choices will also allow you to determine how precisely you have to solve the problem. For example, if your answers are 0, 59, 199, 2,000, and 5,398,700, you know for certain that you can make a very rough estimate and still be correct. If the answers are 3, 4, 5, 6, 7 you know that you had better work the problem out precisely. *Do take the time to check over the answer choices before you begin your calculations.* You will be pleasantly surprised to find out how often you can do away with calculations entirely.

Step Six: *Solve the problem.* Occasionally, you will have to work out the entire problem. Remember, however, that the exam is not written to test your pencil-pushing abilities. The test makers do not want you to spend your time multiplying long numbers or adding many terms. They want to see whether you have the problem solving skills you will need for graduate school. Therefore, if you find you are doing a great many calculations, you are probably missing short cuts or easily estimated solutions.

Using the Answer Choices

You have already learned the importance of looking at the answer choices *before* you begin doing your calculations. Doing so will allow you to eliminate answers that are in the wrong form. Doing so will also allow you to determine how precisely you will have to work the problem. Suppose, however, that looking at the answer choices only tells you that this problem has no short cuts, that you have to work it out entirely.

The answer choices can still help you in such a situation. You can use them to "work backwards" through the problem. For example, consider the ratio problem given at the beginning of this section. You should know (from having studied the review material from Day Three's lesson) that if the ratio of girls to boys is 3:8, there are 3 girls for every 8 boys. Since there are 54 girls, there are 18 groups or sets (54/3) of girls. Therefore, there must be 18 groups or sets of boys. Eighteen sets with 8 boys per set would give you the multiplication problem of 18 × 8. Although this is not an extremely hard problem, why do it? You know that the one's column is 8 × 8 and that 8 × 8 = 64. Therefore, the digit in the one's column must be a 4. Only the correct answer has that digit. This is an example of using the answer choices to prevent pencil-pushing, time-wasting activity on your part.

Traps to Avoid

With the problem solving *questions*, you should be careful to avoid the following traps:

1. *Do not make any assumptions as to what the question is asking.* Be very certain that you know whether you are being asked to find an intermediate step, a total, a percentage, a fraction, a volume, or an area. Determine whether you are being asked to find one value (such as A) or a double value (such as $2A$) or a partial value ($\frac{1}{2}A$). You may wish to circle or underline the exact item you are solving for. For example, in the ratio question given earlier, you may underline "how many boys" to remind yourself that you are not solving for a total number of boys and girls (another typical problem you will find on the exam), but just for the number of boys.

2. *Do not "mentally transfer" information from a preceding problem.* This happens frequently with geometry problems. Just because $X = 40$ in one problem does not mean it equals 40 in another geometry problem. Just because a variable was negative in one problem does not mean it is negative throughout the section. Unless a note tells you that a chart, graph, table, or figure is to be used in more than one problem, approach each problem as if it were the first.

3. *Do not choose "cannot be determined" or "not enough information" unless you are absolutely positive that the problem cannot be solved.* While these answers may be correct on certain problems, if you find that you are choosing them every time you see them, you are probably incorrect.

With the problem solving *answers*, you should be careful to avoid the following traps:

1. *Do not choose the first answer with the correct digits.* For example, answer A may say 64 feet, while answer D says 64 square feet. If you are solving for an area (which is always in square units), you would have to choose answer D. Check your units carefully. Take the few seconds necessary to skim all the answers.

2. *Be careful not to transpose numerals.* To transpose is to reverse the order of, such as writing 28 instead of 82. This error is made frequently by persons rushing to finish the last few problems. Often the answer choices deliberately have "variations on a theme," such as 276 and 267.

3. *Watch the decimal point placement.* An answer of 356.78 is vastly different from an answer of 35.678. Simply because the digits are correct does not mean you may choose an answer and go on to the next problem. Any time you have an answer with a decimal point, you should take extra care to slow down and look at the answer carefully.

Time-saving Suggestions

1. *Preview the problems.* Go directly to those you find relatively simple; save for last those with which you have difficulty. If you find symbolism problems hard but ratio problems simple, go directly to the ratio problems and leave the symbolism problems for the end. This way, if you do not finish the section, the problems you didn't do were the ones you would have done the worst on anyway. You may skip around within a section; just be careful not to lose your place on your answer grid.

2. *Estimate an answer whenever possible.* If you are able to determine that the answer must be within a certain range, you will probably be able to choose an answer from those given without having to do any exact calculations. Whenever possible, work backwards from the answer key rather than working through the whole problem.

3. *Reuse previous calculations.* Occasionally, there is no way to avoid working out specific operations. If you have to multiply 13 × 23 in one problem, chances are you will find that same calculation required later. Try to do your calculations neatly enough so that you can reread them later. Even if you do not have to use that exact same calculation, you may have to make one so close that you can use the previous one as a reference point for an estimation. For example, if you determined that 13 × 23 = 299; you can estimate that 14 × 24 will be just a little larger. You do not have to multiply it out to find it is 336.

Practice Exam: Problem Solving

Please take the following practice exam on the problem solving section. As you learned earlier, the quantitative ability section of the GRE has 30 questions; generally the last 15 of these are problem solving. This practice exam consists of 15 questions with an answer key and explanatory answers following. Score yourself, giving yourself one point for each correct answer. Do *not* subtract points for wrong answers.

DIRECTIONS: Select the best answer to each problem. You may do any scratchwork directly on the exam. Circle the letter that appears before your choice.

1. Eight friends contribute the same amount of money to help pay the rent of a friend who is temporarily broke. When two more friends hear of this generosity, they insist on contributing too, making each person's gift total $80. By how much was each original contributor's donation decreased with the additional funds given by the two friends?

A. $10   D. $35
B. $20   E. $80
C. $25

2. Richard paid $40 each for three shirts, then bought six more when they were reduced 37.5%. What was the average price paid per shirt?

A. $46.90   D. $36.67
B. $41.67   E. $30.00
C. $39.54

3. What is the degree measure of arc AC?

A.   30°   D.   90°
B.   40°   E. 100°
C.   60°

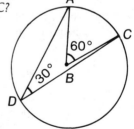

4. How many prime numbers are in the set of numbers from 4 to 25?

   A. 26   D. 11
   B. 25   E. 7
   C. 13

5. The ratio of smokers to nonsmokers in a bar is 4:7. If there are 84 nonsmokers, how many people are there in the bar?

   A. 132   D. 84
   B. 123   E. Cannot be determined
   C. 110

6. What is the approximate measure of an angle in a regular heptagon?

   A. 150°   D. 94°
   B. 129°   E. 60°
   C. 102°

7. $\dfrac{X^{16}}{X^9} =$

   A. X^{25} D. X^2
   B. X^{96} E. X^{169}
   C. X^7

8. $W \# X \# Y \# Z = \dfrac{W}{X} + \dfrac{Y}{Z}$

   What is $2 \# 3 \# 4 \# 5$?

   A. $1\frac{7}{15}$ D. $2\frac{1}{15}$
   B. $2\frac{7}{15}$ E. Cannot be determined
   C. $1\frac{2}{15}$

9. What is the rate of interest on a savings account that made $312 in a six-month period?

   A. 10%   D. 15%
   B. 12%   E. Cannot be determined
   C. 13%

10. Which of the following represents $(a - b)^2$?

    A. $a^2 + 2ab + b^2$ D. $a^2 + b^2$

    B. $a^2 - 2ab + b^2$ E. $a^2 - b^2$

    C. $a^2 + ab + b^2$

11. If an item cost $48.00 and sold for a 12.5% profit, what was the selling price of the item?

    A. $65.00   D. $50.13

    B. $54.00   E. $35.50

    C. $51.50

12. $38X - 14 = 19X + 100$. What is $33\frac{1}{3}\%X$?

    A. 114   D.   6

    B. 38   E.   2

    C. 19

13. Which of the following pieces of information is necessary to find the area of sector *AFB* in circle *F*?

    A. The degree measure of angle *EFB*

    B. The degree measure of angle *ADB*

    C. The radius of the circle

    D. All of the above

    E. None of the above

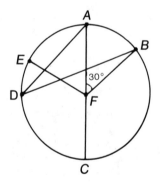

14. Which of the following represents the negative absolute value of negative three?

    A. $|-3|$ D. $-|-3|$

    B. $|3|$ E. None of the above

    C. $-|3|$

15. $10^4 - 10^{-1} =$

    A. 10,001   D. 9,999.9
    B. 10,100   E. 9,999.1
    C. 9,990

ANSWER KEY

1. B	5. A	9. E	13. C
2. E	6. B	10. B	14. D
3. C	7. C	11. B	15. D
4. E	8. A	12. E	

Explanations

1. **(B)** When two friends join eight friends, there are 10 people; if each contributes $80, the total amount contributed is $800. If there were only the original eight friends, the total would still be $800, but each friend would have to pay ⅛, or $100. The difference between the amount paid per person with 10 people ($80) and the amount paid per person with eight people ($100) is $20.

2. **(E)** The first three shirts cost a total of $120. If a shirt is reduced by 37.5%, it is only 62.5% of its original price (because 100% − 37.5% = 62.5%). Since 62.5% = ⅝, you are trying to find what ⅝ of $40 is; it is $25. Six shirts at $25 each cost $150. $150 + $120 = $270. Divide the total, $270, by the number of shirts, 9, to get $30 per shirt.

3. **(C)** The degree measure of an arc is the same as the degree measure of the central angle opposite it. Here, the central angle (the one having the midpoint of the circle as its vertex) is 60°; therefore, the arc is 60° as well.

4. **(E)** Prime numbers are any numbers that may be divided evenly only by themselves and 1. The prime numbers between 4 and 25 are (5, 7, 11, 13, 17, 19, 23).

5. **(A)** Think of the ratio as telling you how many persons are in a set; there are 4 persons in a set of smokers and 7 persons in a set of nonsmokers. Since there are 84 nonsmokers, there are

12 *sets* (84/7) of nonsmokers. There must then be 12 sets of smokers. With 4 people to a set, there are 48 (4 × 12) smokers. 84 + 48 = 132.

6. **(B)** Find the total degree measure of all of the interior angles with the formula $(S - 2)(180°)$, with S representing the number of sides of the figure. A heptagon has 7 sides; therefore you multiply $(7 - 2)$ or 5 by 180° to get 900°. Since a *regular* polygon has all equal sides and all equal angles, divide the total by the number of angles. $900/7 = 128.57$ or approximately 129°.

7. **(C)** When dividing like bases with different exponents (the X is the base; the number is the exponent), subtract the exponents. $16 - 9 = 7$.

8. **(A)** The # is a symbol. The first part of the problem tells you how to use the symbol; you make a fraction of the first two numbers, then add it to a fraction made of the second two numbers. You may also think of this problem as substituting the 2 for the W, the 3 for the X, the 4 for the Y, and the 5 for the Z. This gives you $\frac{2}{3} + \frac{4}{5}$. Use the common denominator of 15 to get $\frac{10}{15} + \frac{12}{15} = \frac{22}{15}$ or $1\frac{7}{15}$.

9. **(E)** The formula needed here is $I = PRT$ (Interest equals Principal times Rate times Time). Here, you are given the interest earned and the time but are not given either the principal or the rate. To get the rate, you would need to be given the principal. Since the principal is not given here, the answer cannot be determined.

10. **(B)** Work through the problem as shown below, taking one variable at a time and multiplying it by the others. Note that $-ab$ and $-ba$ are the same; any two numbers may be multiplied in any order (such as 6×5 or 5×6).

$$(a - b)(a - b)$$
$$a \cdot a = a^2$$
$$a \cdot -b = -ab$$
$$-b \cdot a = -ba$$
$$\underline{-b \cdot -b = +b^2}$$
$$a^2 - 2ab + b^2$$

11. **(B)** The formula needed here is $S = C + P$, Sales price equals Cost plus Profit. The profit is 12.5%, which is the same as ⅛. One-eighth of the cost is $6. Add the profit of $6 to the cost of $48 to get the selling price of $54. Note that you could automatically have eliminated answer E. The selling price must be *more* than the cost, since the question tells you that a profit (rather than a loss) occurred.

12. **(E)** This is a simple algebra question that you could easily have missed had you been careless and not read what the question wanted you to solve for. You are not giving an answer of "$X = \ldots$" but an answer of "33⅓% $X = \ldots$" First, find for X. Move all the X terms to one side and all the non-X terms to the other. Move the $19X$ to the left, making it $-19X$ (remember that when you move a term from one side of the equal sign to the other, you change its sign—a positive becomes a negative and a negative becomes a positive). Move the -14 to the right of the equal sign, making it $+14$. Combine like terms: $38X - 19X = 19X$. $100 + 14 = 114$. (Note that 114 is one of the trap answers.) Divide both sides through by 19 in order to get an X by itself. $\frac{19X}{19} = X$; $\frac{114}{19} = 6$. You now know that $X = 6$; However, remember that the question wants to know what 33⅓% X is. Since 33⅓% is the same as ⅓, you can determine that ⅓ X is the same as $\frac{X}{3}$, or $\frac{6}{3} = 2$. You didn't fall into the trap and put answer D, did you?

13. **(C)** In order to find the area of a sector, you need to have two pieces of information: the fraction that the sector is of the area of the circle (found by knowing the fraction that the central angle is of the total degree measure of the circle) and the area of the circle. In this case you have the former and only need the latter. Answer A is incorrect because the sector *AFB* has nothing to do with angle *EFB*. If you wanted to find the area of sector *EFB*, rather than of sector *AFB*, you would need that angle. Here, it is irrelevant. Answer B is a little more useful, but not *necessary*. Since angle *ADB* has the same intercepted arc (arc *AB*) as angle *AFB*, you know that angle *ADB* has ½ the degree measure of angle *AFB*. If you didn't know the degree measure of angle *AFB*, knowing the degree measure of angle *ADB* would be critical. However, since the problem

tells you the measure of *AFB* is 30°, you don't need to know the measure of angle *ADB*. Answer C is correct. Since you still must find the area of the circle, you have to have some linear measurement that would allow you to find it. You could have the radius or the diameter or the longest chord. With the radius you could find the area and multiply it by the fraction that angle *AFB* is of the circle.

14. **(D)** The absolute value is the magnitude of a number, the number of actual units regardless of the positive or negative status. Absolute value is represented by two vertical lines, such that |5| would be read as "the absolute value of 5." Absolute values are always given as positive. |−5| would be read as "the absolute value of negative 5," but the answer would be 5, not negative 5. Answer A represents the absolute value of negative 3. Answer B represents the absolute value of positive 3. Answer C represents the negative absolute value of positive 3. Answer D is correct; it represents the negative absolute value of negative 3.

15. **(D)** Ten to the fourth is 10,000. Ten to the negative first is the same as $\frac{1}{10}$, or .1. $10,000 - .1 = 9,999.9$. Note how the other answers are all devious; if you chose any of them, you probably tried to do this problem too quickly. Remember that you should look at the answer key *before* doing the problem. Had you done so in this instance, you would have noted that the answers are all pretty close and rather tricky. Because of this, you should have slowed down, taken the time to write out the problem and actually do the math visually, rather than just in your head.

SCORE: NUMBER RIGHT:

NO PENALTY FOR WRONG ANSWERS

Hour Two: Data Interpretation

Set Your Clock. You will have a full hour to complete this section. Since the questions are in the standard multiple choice format and you have already learned the background mathematics required to perform the calculations (percentages, ratios, and other basic arithmetic functions), concentrate on understanding the tables and graphs themselves, identifying the various types and the procedures used to interpret them.

The Question Style

Data Interpretation questions ask you to understand tables and graphs and answer questions based on information given in them. Above the table or graph will be a direction such as: "Questions 30–32 refer to the following table" or "Questions 35–40 refer to the following data." Be sure to note exactly which questions require use of the graph.

It is more common to have the data interpretation questions in the problem solving format than in the quantitative comparisons format. That is, the questions following the table or graph will usually be in the multiple-choice format. If a quantitative comparisons question is asked, the table or graph involved will usually be very simple; remember, quantitative comparisons questions do not ask you for a specific solution to a problem but only for a comparison of the magnitudes of two quantities.

Interpreting the Table or Graph

1. *Read the title.* The title limits the scope of the graph and is critical. For example, a title might be: "Number of deaths from cancer in America, 1980–1990." If the question asks you about the number of deaths from accidents or some cause other than cancer, you cannot answer. If the question asks you the number of cancer cases—as opposed to *deaths* from cancer—you cannot answer. If the question asks you the number of deaths from

cancer in South America or in years other than 1980–1990, you cannot answer.

2. *Read the titles of the columns of the table or the titles of the axes of the graphs.* Consider these "subtitles" just as important—and occasionally as tricky—as the title of the entire figure. Identify the units of measurement used. For example, if the left axis of a graph shows a 10, is that ten (10), ten hundred (1,000), ten thousand (10,000), ten hundred thousand (1,000,000) or ten million (10,000,000)? NOTE: Occasionally, there is an "extra axis" to the far right. An example of a graph with one of these is given in the practice exam. Read both the left and the right sides and note whether they are in different units of measurement (e.g., the left axis may be in tens of thousands while the right axis is in thousands).

3. *Read the key.* Close to the graph will be a key that explains what the coloring of the graph represents (e.g., the shaded portion may mean men under 30, the striped portion men between 30 and 50, and the unshaded portion men over 50). The key is as important in limiting the graph as is the title. For example, the key may indicate that the graph covers only men; a question on women would have to be answered with "It cannot be determined from the information given."

4. *Note any additional information.* Sometimes, below the graph or to the side is an essential piece of information such as: "Total = $400,000." Unless you read this information, you cannot answer a question that asks for a specific number when the graph features only percentages.

Answering the Questions

In general, questions following a table or graph go from easy to hard. The first question after the graph may be answered quickly merely by looking at the graph. The purpose of the question is to determine whether you understand the layout of the graph, whether you have noted the axes. For example, a typical first question might be: "In which year were sales the highest?" or "In how many years did sales exceed $3,000,000?" Do not read any tricks into the first question; it usually is quite straightforward.

Occasionally, there are "nested graphs," or a graph within a graph (you will see one of these on the practice exam). This occurs when you have two graphs, one of which is a "blow up" of a part of the first graph. For example, the first graph might be sales for the whole company, broken down into divisions. Division A makes 20% of the company's sales. Then the second graph features only Division A. If 50% of Division A's sales are of clocks, remember that clocks are 50% of 20% of the total, or half of 20%, or 10%. That means that clocks represent 10% of total sales for the company, not 50%. When you see two tables or graphs, note whether they are independent or dependent.

Identify exactly what the question is asking for before you begin performing your calculations. The point of the data interpretation questions is not to have you do a great deal of addition or multiplication, but to determine whether you are able to comprehend a graph. That means that occasionally the questions may not be answerable or may be answered with a very rough estimate. For example, if the question asks you for an average, do not immediately begin adding all the columns and then dividing by the number of columns; that much pencil-pushing is unnecessary. Look at the graph. The average must be between the high and low points; you may be able to estimate it at a glance. Use the answer choices and the process of elimination.

Traps to Avoid

With the tables and graphs themselves, you should be careful to avoid the following traps:

1. *Do not use outside knowledge, other than common sense and everyday facts (such as the number of days in a year).* All of the information you need to answer a question is given in the graph; if it is not, choose the answer, "It cannot be determined from the

information given." You are not expected to know the GNP of China or the percentage of sales that General Motors has in Peru.

2. *Do not try to read every piece of information on the graph.* The majority of information on any table or graph is not necessary to answer the questions. Read only the title, axes, key and notes. Do not go to the graph and mutter to yourself: "In 1973, sales of Division A were $5,000,000; in 1973, sales of Division B were . . ."

3. *Note whether the graph is in units or percentages.* This is one of the most common traps. Some graphs are in percentages; you cannot answer a question asking for a quantity unless you have a total given somewhere. Usually, the total is in a note below the graph. If you are told "Total Sales = $14,000,000," only then can you use the graph to determine how much was sold (as opposed to what percentage) in 1985.

With the questions, avoid the following traps:

1. *Do not read more into a question than is given there.* Some of the questions, especially those immediately following the graph, require very simple answers that may be obtained just by looking at the graph. Do not perform calculations unless necessary.

2. *Note the specific information requested and the form the question wants.* For example, the question may not ask for an average per se but for how many years are above the average. One of the "trap" answer choices is almost certainly going to be the average. Answer what the question is asking.

3. *Give the answer in the form requested.* The question may ask for the quantity of sales; do not choose an answer that gives a percentage. Doublecheck the axes; as mentioned previously, they may be given in numerals that represent other quantities (for example, "10" actually may mean "ten hundreds of thousands," or 1,000,000).

Time-saving Suggestions

1. *Use the side of your answer grid as a straightedge to estimate whenever possible.* Instead of performing calculations, hold the paper so that you can see a "pattern," or estimate an average. If the question is at the end of the cluster (say the fifth question out of five pertaining to that graph), you may in fact need to do the mathematics. However, if it is an earlier question, often an estimation is satisfactory.

2. *Use information from a previous question on this graph to help you answer the next question.* If you do calculations, do them neatly. This interim information may be helpful to you in answering a more involved question later; sometimes, questions based on the same graph do build upon one another. You do not want to have to redo the same calculations.

3. *Check the answer key at intervals before performing calculations to obtain a precise answer.* For example, if you are asked to find a percentage, but come up with an answer of $\frac{1}{17}$, you do not have to divide to find a precise percentage. The answer choices will be spaced far enough apart to let you estimate ($\frac{1}{20} = \frac{1}{5} = 20\%$; this answer should be a little greater than that).

Practice Exam: Data Interpretation

Please take the following practice exam on the data interpretation questions. As you learned earlier, data interpretation is usually a part of the problem solving section, though there may occasionally be a graph or table given in the quantitative comparisons material. The entire GRE math section has 30 questions, both quantitative comparisons and problem solving. This abbreviated practice exam features 15 data interpretation questions in the problem solving format. The answer key and explanatory answers follow. Score yourself, giving yourself one point for each correct answer. Do *not* subtract points for wrong answers.

Questions 1–3 Refer to Table 1

TABLE 1

Expenditures for Raw Materials—Guthrie Group, Inc. (in tens of thousands of dollars)

	1987	1988	1989
Beads	6.7	6.9	7.4
Semi-precious stones	3.8	3.2	3.6
Fabric	9.1	9.8	12.4
Miscellaneous	1.0	1.3	0.7

1. Fabric expenditures from 1988 to 1989

   A. increased by 10%
   B. increased by 18%
   C. increased by 27%
   D. remained approximately the same
   E. decreased by 27%

2. What percentage of the total expenditures for the Guthrie Group 1987–1980 was spent on other than beads?

   A. 7.4%
   B. 21%

C. 44.9%
D. 60%
E. 68%

3. The amount spent for fabric in 1987 and misc. in 1989 was how much greater than the amount spent for semi-precious stones in 1988 and beads in 1989?

A. $8
B. $80
C. $800
D. $8,000
E. $80,000

Questions 4–7 Refer to Dickstein Academy Graph

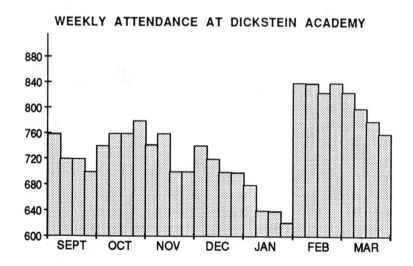

WEEKLY ATTENDANCE AT DICKSTEIN ACADEMY

4. What was the lowest attendance during the months shown?

   A. 600
   B. 620
   C. 640
   D. 660
   E. 680

5. For how many weeks Sept–March were fewer than 700 students attending class in one week?

   A. 10
   B. 7
   C. 5
   D. 4
   E. 0

6. The average number of students per week Oct–Nov was

   A. 700
   B. 710.5
   C. 720
   D. 742.5
   E. 751.5

7. The lowest number of students attending for one week on the graph is what percentage of attendance for the year?

   A. 620
   B. 100
   C. 70
   D. 6.2
   E. It cannot be determined from the information given.

EXPENSES OF SHAYNA CORP

OVERALL EXPENSES

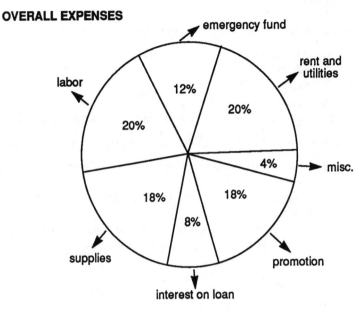

TOTAL =$5,000,000

LABOR COSTS

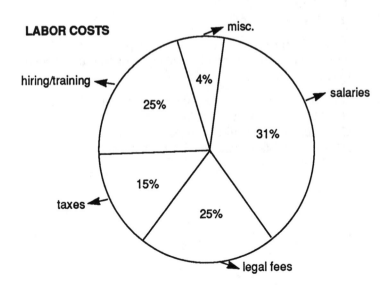

Questions 8–10 Refer to the Shayna Corp Graphs

8. According to the graphs, legal fees represent a labor cost of

   A. $5,000,000
   B. $2,500,000
   C. $250,000
   D. $25,000
   E. It cannot be determined from the information given.

9. Which of the following statements is true about misc. costs?

   I. Misc. costs for the project are equal to misc. costs for labor
   II. Misc. costs for the project are five times misc. costs for labor
   III. Misc. costs for labor are 5% of misc. costs for the project
   IV. Misc. costs for labor are proportionally equal to misc. costs for the project

   A. I only
   B. I and II only
   C. II and III only
   D. II and IV only
   E. I, II, and IV only

10. If the hiring/training share of labor costs were to double while total costs remained constant, which of the following would be true?

    A. Labor costs would be 50% of total costs
    B. Labor costs would be 25% of total costs
    C. Labor costs would be 10% of total costs
    D. Labor costs would be 5% of total costs
    E. None of the above

CAUSES OF EMPLOYEE DEPARTURE

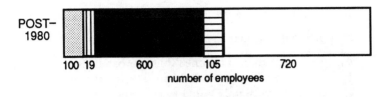

POST–
1980

| 100 | 19 | 600 | 105 | 720 |

number of employees

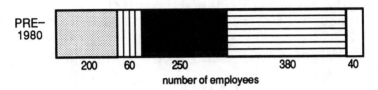

PRE–
1980

| 200 | 60 | 250 | 380 | 40 |

number of employees

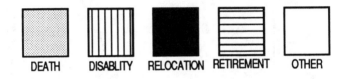

DEATH   DISABLITY   RELOCATION   RETIREMENT   OTHER

Questions 11–13 Refer to the Employee Departure Graphs

11. Post-1980, approximately what percentage of employee departure was due to relocation?

   A. 600%
   B. 60%
   C. 39%
   D. 6%
   E. 3.9%

12. According to the graph, the number of people working in the company pre-1980

   A. was 166% the number working there post-1980
   B. was 60% the number working there post-1980
   C. was 614 less than those working there post-1980

    D.   was approximately equal to those working there post-1980

    E.   It cannot be determined from the information given.

13. Proportionally, departure due to retirement pre-1980

    A.   was more than five times that in post-1980

    B.   was approximately ⅕ that post-1980

    C.   was approximately equal to that post-1980

    D.   was 15% greater than that post-1980

    E.   was 1.5% greater than that post-1980

Questions 14–15 Refer to the Kithawker Graph

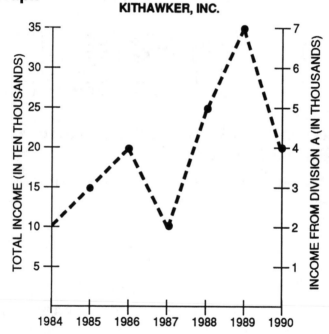

KITHAWKER, INC.

14. In 1985, income from division A was approximately

    A. $1,500,000

    B. $1,000,000

    C. $3,000

D. $2,000

E. It cannot be determined from the information given.

15. In 1988, the income from division A was what percent of the total income of Kithawker, Inc.?

A. 200%

B. 20%

C. 2%

D. .02%

E. .002%

ANSWER KEY

1. C	6. D	11. C
2. E	7. E	12. E
3. D	8. C	13. A
4. B	9. D	14. C
5. D	10. B	15. C

Explanations

1. **(C)** You can immediately eliminate answers (D) and (E); it is obvious that expenditures for fabric increased. To find percent of increase, take the number increase (from 9.8 to 12.4 is 2.6) and put it over the original whole, what you are increasing from. 2.6/9.8 is approximately .27, or 27%. NOTE: The percentage of increase (or decrease) formula is an important one and should be memorized. It will be useful for both graphs and general math problems. % increase or decrease = number increase or decrease/original whole.

2. **(E)** Find the total expenditures by adding all the numbers: 65.9. Subtract the expenditure for beads from the total: 65.9 − 21 = 44.9. A percentage is part over whole: 44.9/65.9 = .68 = 68%.

3. **(D)** This is a simple, read-the-table problem. Add 9.1 + .7 = 9.8. Add 3.2 + 7.4 = 10.6. 10.6 − 9.8 = .8 Now, you need to remember that the table is in tens of thousands of dollars: .8 × 10,000 = 8,000.

4. **(B)** The attendance during the last week of January was 620.

5. **(D)** Look at the graph. There are four weeks, all in January, in which the line drops below 700.

6. **(D)** You could do this problem the long way, adding all the numbers $(740 + 760 + 760 + 780 + 740 + 760 + 700 + 700 = 5940)$ and dividing by 8 (the number of items). Or you could look at the answer key and see that all the answer choices are in the seven hundreds, making the hundreds digit irrelevant to this problem. It is much easiser just to add the last two digits of the numbers: $40 + 60 + 60 + 80 + 40 + 60 + 0 + 0 = 340$. Divide that by 8 to get 42.5.

7. **(E)** This is as close to a "trick" question as the exam may get. The chart shows *only* the months Sept–Mar, not the entire year. Therefore, we do not have enough information to answer the question. (If you skipped this question, thinking it would take a lot of "pencil-pushing" to add up all the individual weeks' attendance, you fell into the trap. Remember, very few questions require many time-consuming calculations. Your interpretive skills are being tested, not your adding and dividing abilities.)

8. **(C)** With this type of dual graph, you should note that the entire second graph is 20% of the first graph. Since the first graph is $5,000,000, the total for the second graph is $1,000,000. On the exam, it would be wise to write that under the second graph immediately. Legal fees are 25% of the labor total, or one-fourth of a million dollars, $250,000.

9. **(D)** This is a tricky question. Keep in mind that the entire first graph is five times the second graph. Since both graphs show 4% misc. costs, the project misc. costs are five times the labor misc. costs (statement II). They are proportionately equal (4%) but not equal in dollars (4% of $5,000,000 versus 4% of $1,000,000). Statement III is misleading; 5% is one-twentieth, not one-fifth.

10. **(B)** Hiring/training costs are currently 25% of $1,000,000 = $250,000. To double them, add another $250,000. That brings the overall labor costs to $1,250,000. That is 25% of the (unchanged) total costs $(1,250,000/5,000,000 = .25 = 25\%)$.

11. **(C)** A percentage is part over whole. Find the whole by adding $100 + 19 + 600 + 105 + 720 = 1544$. Relocation $= 600$. $600/1544 = .39 = 39\%$. NOTE: You did not have to do the actual division; look at the answer choices. Since 600 is less than half of 1544, the answer cannot be 60%. Both 6% and 3.9% are much too small; the correct answer is a logical estimate.

12. **(E)** We know nothing about the number of people *working* at any time, pre- or post-1980. All we know is the number of employee departures. It is important to read the titles of the graphs so that you are aware of what is and what is NOT covered by the graph.

13. **(A)** Find the proportion that retirements were pre-1980: 380/930 (part over whole) $= .41$. Find the proportion that retirements were

post-1980: 105/1544 = .07. Before doing any more calculations, look at the answer choices. Only choice (A) is possible.

14. (**C**) With a dual axis graph (that is, both the right and left axes are labelled) be certain to look at the correct axis to answer the question. Look at 1985, then look to the right to the 3. Since the Division A income is in thousands, this is $3,000.

15. (**C**) In 1988, Division A income was 5, or $5,000. Total income was 25, or $250,000 (remember that the left axis is in tens of thousands of dollars). To find a percentage, put part over whole: 5,000/250,000 = .02 or 2%. If you chose (D), you fell into the trap. .02% is actually .0002, not .02.

SCORE: NUMBER RIGHT:

NO PENALTY FOR WRONG ANSWERS

5.

DAY FIVE

Hour One: Logical Reasoning

Set Your Clock. *You will have a full hour to review the first of two types of analytical questions you will find on the GRE. The logical reasoning questions are more familiar and relatively easier to understand and answer than are the second type of analytical questions, analytical reasoning (which will be discussed in the second hour of today's lesson). Therefore, if you finish this section early, you may wish to spend extra time on the second hour's lesson.*

The Question Style

Logical reasoning questions look rather like short reading comprehension questions. You will be given a sentence, a short paragraph, or a one- or two-paragraph passage. Following each sentence, paragraph, or passage will be a brief question with five answer choices.

For this type of analytical ability question, you will not need to make drawings or do any scratchwork. Basic reading and deductive skills are tested.

A typical logical reasoning question looks like this:

> Drinking soft drinks with caffeine makes you nervous. My best friend drinks a full six-pack of cola drinks a day and she is the jitteriest person I know.

Which of the following statements (if true) most weakens the conclusion given in the passage above?

A. Since I have begun drinking cola drinks, I have noticed I am talking faster.
B. My parents drink decaffeinated coffee and are very calm, tranquil people.

C. My brother drinks a lot of milk and is a very nervous person.

D. My uncle is an alcoholic who never drinks soft drinks but is still a nervous wreck.

E. Most of my friends drink more colas than I do but have not become any more "hyper" than usual.

Format

The entire analytical ability section of the GRE consists of 25 questions which you are to answer in 30 minutes. Usually, anywhere from 6 to 10 of those questions are logical reasoning while the remaining 15 to 19 are analytical reasoning. There is no special order in which the two question styles are presented. Unlike the math section, in which it is customary to have all of the quantitative comparison questions given first, followed by all of the problem solving questions, the logical reasoning and analytical reasoning questions are mixed together.

The Basic Logical Reasoning Questions

There are several basic questions which you may be given. While there are many variations on these, if you understand and can read and answer questions in the styles given below, you should do very well on this portion of the exam.

1. Styles and Methods of Reasoning

In this type of question, you are given a paragraph which argues or reasons to a conclusion. You are to determine what style or method of reasoning is used. For example, did the author give a hypothesis, then give fact after fact after fact to support that hypothesis? Did the author first give a number of facts and then combine them to reach a conclusion? Did the author give a pro argument, then a con, then a pro, then a con, leading to a conclusion? There are many different styles of reasoning a writer may use. Remember that you are not required to draw a style out of thin air; you are given five answer choices. Read the passage, try to *predict* what you think the style is, then look to see whether your answer is given. If your answer (or one very similar) is not given, use the answers to see which one you think best describes the way the author made his or her point.

> EXAMPLE: I know that most graduate schools look very carefully at the GRE scores. I have a friend who did very poorly during all four years of college, but got a great GRE score and was admitted to graduate programs everywhere. I have another friend who was a straight A student as an undergraduate but got nervous while taking the GRE. She got a terrible score and was rejected by every graduate program to which she had applied!

Which of the following best describes the author's form of reasoning in the passage above?

A. She gives facts leading to a conclusion.
B. She states a conclusion and supports it with facts.
C. She proposes a hypothesis and gives the steps she used to develop that hypothesis.
D. She states a conclusion developed by others and gives evidence to rebut it.
E. She gives a chronological history or background of events that caused her to reach a conclusion.

Which answer did you choose? If you chose B you were correct. If you chose C, you chose the *second best* answer, but still missed the question. The key to the right answer is the word "conclusion." The author states in the first sentence that she *knows* how important GRE scores are. She is not tentatively proposing a hypothesis; she is dogmatically stating a conclusion. She then gives the facts that support her conclusion. Note that it makes no difference whether her conclusion is, in fact, correct. You are concerned with the author's method of reasoning, not the validity or invalidity of her conclusion. Answer C is rather sneaky. Apart from the fact that the statement of the author is not a hypothesis, you could eliminate this answer because no "steps" were given. That is, the author did not tell you what she did first, then did second, etc. You are told *facts*, not *steps*.

Did you notice that answer A at first appears correct, but is backwards? If you chose it, you were careless and didn't read the rest of the answer choices. Be especially wary of "backwards" or "reversed" answers of this sort.

2. Inference

The inference question requires you to determine what inference or inferences may logically be made from the passage. In other words, you have to decide what you may logically conclude using information given or by reading "between the lines" of the passage.

> EXAMPLE: Studying in a room with a radio blaring in the background may cause a lack of concentration leading to an incomplete understanding of the material being read. Studies have shown that persons who study with the radio blaring tend to do poorly on exams. However, recent studies have also shown that persons who study to music also tend to study for shorter periods of time than do persons who study in quiet environments.

Which of the following is the most logical inference to draw from the information given above?

A. Shorter study time may be a contributing factor to poor scores.
B. Deaf people do better on exams than people who can hear.
C. Persons who blare radios always study for shorter periods of time than do persons who play their radios at normal volume.
D. Persons who study without music learn more rapidly than do persons who study with music.
E. Time is the most significant factor in determining who will do well or poorly on exams.

The correct answer is A. An *inference* is a conclusion that you, the reader, may *logically* draw from the information given. The passage tells you that people who study to loud music may do worse on exams than people who don't study to such music; but then it goes on to state that there is possibly another cause, the fact that those music aficionados tend to study for shorter periods of time than do the others. You may therefore draw an inference that perhaps the noise itself is not the only reason that one group of studiers does more poorly than another; perhaps the *time* spent studying is another factor.

Did you get tricked into choosing answer C? Answer C is not the best answer for more than one reason. First, the word "always" should immediately eliminate it from your consideration. Rarely can you make an inference that is *always* true about anything. Secondly, you are being asked for an inference, and the passage tells you that (according to studies), persons with blaring radios study for shorter periods of time than do persons without such distractions. Do not confuse what you infer with what you are actually given.

3. Similar Reasoning

You may be given a short passage of one or two sentences that uses a particular form of reasoning to make its point. Then you are asked which of the five answer choices has that same reasoning. In order to answer the question, you must, therefore, be able to identify the form of reasoning used in the passage.

> EXAMPLE: All of the makeup artists on Hollywood's biggest films use Beauty Gel brand makeup; therefore, Beauty Gel brand makeup is the best makeup available.

The reasoning above is most similar to that found in which of the following?

A. No hairdressers use razors to cut hair anymore; therefore, scissors are the best means of cutting hair.
B. All Rhodes scholars use Mr. Hart's method of speed reading; therefore, Mr. Hart's method is preferable to any other method available.
C. All the criminals in County Jail read dirty magazines; therefore, reading dirty magazines will make you a criminal.

D. The best rice is Brand X; all four-star restaurants serve it regularly.

E. Only the very wealthy can afford to wear designer fashions, therefore, designer fashions are the best

The correct answer is B. To answer this type of question, first *identify the reasoning* used. The passage is stating that because prominent, important, respected people in that particular field (one assumes Hollywood makeup artists know what they're doing) use a particular product, that product must be the best product available. The reasoning in answer B is the same. Because the persons most prestigious in their fields (Rhodes scholars are among the nation's most elite and respected scholars) use a particular product (here, a method of reading), that product must be the best available.

Note the reasoning in the other answers. In A, you are assuming that just because one method is not good, another method must be good. This is not the same reasoning used in the original passage. Answer C is totally different as well. It has the reasoning that just because one group does something, doing that same thing will make you a member of the group. Answer D might have tricked you. The reasoning is correct, but it is reversed. It first tells you that something is the best, then says that it must be the best because the best people in that field use it. Answer E is close, but incorrect. It states that because only the elite group (here, the wealthy people) can afford to use something, that something must be the best. There is a difference between the elite group using something that everyone can use, and the elite group using something that only it can use.

4. Strengthen or Weaken Argument

One of the most common questions in this portion of the exam is one that asks which of the answer choices most *strengthens* or most *weakens* the conclusion given in the passage. First you must determine the conclusion. Then you should try to *predict* what statement you would make, what fact you would give, to support or refute that conclusion.

EXAMPLE: Discrimination is rampant in Mythland. Last year only 3% of those working in prestigious positions were green people.

Which of the following statements, if true, would most strengthen the conclusion given above?

A. Green people hold positions of trust in other governments.
B. Green people make up over 25% of the population of Mythland.
C. Green people are just as reliable as anyone else, according to recent statistics.
D. Purple people receive higher salaries in Mythland than do green people.
E. Purple people are better suited for prestigious positions than are green people.

The correct answer is B. First, identify the conclusion. It is that discrimination is rampant. You should now *predict* what type of statement you would make to support such a conclusion. You could best support the statement by giving facts and figures to show such discrimination. The passage tells you that only 3% of the prestigious positions were held by green people; if you know that green people make up significantly more than 3% of the population, you support the conclusion that they are being discriminated against.

Take a look at the incorrect answers. A and C may be true, but they do not *specifically* support the statement that there is discrimination in Mythland. Just because other countries have more green people employed in prestigious positions does not necessarily mean there is discrimination in Mythland (perhaps green people are only a small fraction of the population of Mythland after all). Just because green people are reliable does not mean there are enough of them for the 3% figure to imply blatant discrimination.

Answer D may be considered the second best answer. It does support the conclusion that there is discrimination; however, it is not as strong of a support as is the correct answer. (Perhaps purple people earn higher salaries because they work harder or go into specific jobs by choice.) Answer E is actually a *weakening* statement. If you can indeed show that purple people are better suited for such positions, then having few green people in them is not discrimination, it is common sense.

5. Assumptions

You may be asked to determine the assumption the writer made. You will have to read the passage and ask yourself what general background facts, what theories or concepts, the author assumed while he or she was writing. Generally, with this type of question, you will not predict an answer; you will use the answer choices given, going through each one to determine whether it states a fact or concept which the author automatically accepted.

> EXAMPLE: The city commissioner told the press that, as mayor, he will crack down on organized crime by increasing the police department budget and assigning more officers to street duty.

The city commissioner assumes all of the following except:

A. Crime would be reduced if there were more police on the street.
B. He will be elected mayor.
C. Citizens want to see a decrease in organized crime activities.
D. Organized crime will be wiped out, given sufficient time and personnel.
E. The mayor will have influence on the police department budget.

The correct answer is D. This answer is what is known as an *absolute*. "Wiped out" means able to be eliminated entirely, able to be eradicated completely. The commissioner does not assume this; he only assumes that he can "crack down" on organized crime, possibly reducing it.

Each of the other answers is a statement it is reasonable to conclude the speaker assumed. For answer A, it is logical that the speaker thought that more police would help reduce crime; otherwise he would not discuss reducing crime and increasing the number of police officers in the same context. Answer B is perhaps the most logical assumption. The city commissioner would not be discussing what he will do as mayor unless he assumes he will become mayor. C is also a logical assumption. A candidate for mayor is going to talk about doing what the people want done. The speaker must assume that people want crime reduced or he wouldn't be proposing a program to do so. Finally, answer E is a logical assumption. The speaker would not be discussing how, as mayor, he will increase the police budget, unless he assumes that he will have the authority to do so, or at least have some influence on the budget. NOTE: *None* of these assumptions necessarily has to be true (perhaps the mayor has nothing to do with the budget in that particular city); the speaker only has to *assume* they are true.

6. Examples

You may be given a sentence or a quotation and asked what it is an *example* of. For example, if you are given Nathan Hale's heroic statement that he regretted he had but one life to give for his country, that would be an example of patriotism.

> EXAMPLE: When caught looking at the exam paper of the student next to him, Harold was asked why he wasn't doing his own work. He replied, "Because I was sharing the expertise of my colleague to my unilateral advantage."

Harold's statement is an example of

A. assuming facts not in evidence
B. restating the obvious
C. proposing a hypothesis based on illogical or incorrect facts
D. changing the subject
E. refuting a conclusion

The correct answer is B. The passage tells you that Harold was caught in the act of cheating, of looking at someone else's work.

His statement merely said the same thing, that he was "sharing" someone else's work. He said it with finesse, but he said only what had already been noted.

The incorrect answers are not even close on this question. Answer A is illogical; no facts are assumed at all. Answer C is incorrect because Harold proposes no hypothesis. Answer D is wrong because Harold, rather than changing the subject, makes things worse by reiterating the teacher's statement. Answer E is incorrect; no conclusion was made in the first place, let alone refuted.

Summary. While there are, of course, other types of questions you may be asked, these six are ones that tend to show up frequently on the GRE. Make certain that you can recognize each style, and know how best to approach it. Take the time to go through the explanations of the *wrong* answers given above so that you recognize traps you want to avoid. You may find on this portion of the exam that it is easier to note and eliminate the wrong answers than to deduce the right answer. Remember also there is no penalty for guessing.

Traps to Avoid

1. *Do not predict the question, only the answer.* In other words, try reading the question *before* the passage. If you read the passage first, you may wrongly assume what you are going to be asked. You may think that you are going to be asked a question on the assumptions the author makes, while in fact you are asked which statement most strengthens the author's conclusion. If you try to predict the question, you will waste time twice, first in making your prediction and second in having to go back and reread the passage in light of the actual question to be answered. *Read the question first, then read the passage, then answer the question.*

2. *Do not misread the question.* This means that you should note whether the question wants you to find which statement *supports, negates, strengthens,* or *weakens* the author's conclusion. It is very easy to misread a question, and choose an answer that supports a

conclusion when you were asked to find an answer that weakens a conclusion. As you read the question, circle or underline the key word, such as "support," "negate," "strengthen," or "weaken."

3. *Read all the answer choices.* In these types of questions, more than one answer may seem correct. While there can be only one correct answer, of course, you may sincerely feel that two or more answers are "good." If you read only until you find a "good" answer, you may miss a "better" and a "best" answer later.

Time-saving Suggestions

1. *Do all the logical reasoning questions first.* As you learned before, the logical reasoning questions are sprinkled among the analytical reasoning questions in this section. Because the logical reasoning questions are generally easier to read and understand, and quicker to answer than the analytical reasoning questions, try to do them first. Just be careful not to lose your place on your answer grid when you skip around within a section.

2. *Predict an answer whenever possible.* As you went through each of the six general question types given above, you learned when predicting is useful and when it is a waste of time. Often, predicting will save you much time, as you will generally see your answer as soon as you look for it. When you see the answer you've predicted, you won't have to waste time agonizing over the other answers that all seem good. Trust yourself. Generally your own predicted answer is right.

3. *Guess, guess, guess.* There is no penalty for guessing. If you don't understand the question, it is tempting to reread it over and over. However, after you have read it twice, guess at an answer and go on to the next question. Some logical reasoning questions are intentionally written to be confusing or thought provoking (remember that they are testing your ability to analyze difficult information). While you should be able to answer the questions based on the knowledge you acquire from this book, if you hit a snag, go on. Each question counts the same; don't spend so much time trying to get one difficult one right that you never make it to three or four simple questions later in the section.

Practice Exam: Logical Reasoning

Please take the following practice exam on the logical reasoning portion of the analytical ability section. As you learned earlier, the whole analytical ability section has 25 questions; 6 to 10 of those questions will be logical reasoning and the rest will be analytical reasoning. The following exam covers only logical reasoning questions. This practice exam consists of 10 questions with an answer key and explanatory answers following. Score yourself, giving yourself one point for each correct answer. Do *not* subtract points for wrong answers.

NOTE: Since the logical reasoning and analytical reasoning questions are intermingled in the analytical ability section on the actual exam, the directions below would apply to both question types. Here, you may ignore the statement about creating a diagram or chart; it is irrelevant for the logical reasoning questions.

DIRECTIONS: Each question or set of questions below is based on a short passage or upon a set of conditions given. You may draw a diagram or chart to help you answer some questions, Choose the best answer for each question. Circle the letter that appears before your answer.

1. The most popular men in school are Roger, Frank, and Eustace. Right behind them in popularity are Rashid, Gene, Julio, and Emilio. All of these men are on the football team. If I join the football team, my popularity is bound to rise.

Which of the following best describes the author's form of reasoning in the passage above?

A. He states a hypothesis then gives examples in support of it.
B. He gives an opinion, buttressing it with examples.

C. He makes a deduction based on individual examples.
D. He states an exception to prove a rule.
E. He states a commonly accepted theory and refutes it.

2. After seeing Jake's grades go from C−'s to B+'s after a summer of intensive tutoring, Jacob decided to use money from his savings account to pay Jake's tutor to work with him again.

Which is the most logical inference to draw from the information given above?

A. Jake's grades improved because of the tutoring.
B. Jacob thought that Jake's grades improved because of the tutoring.
C. Jake's grades would have remained the same without the tutoring.
D. Jacob's grades will not improve without tutoring.
E. Jake is more intelligent than Jacob.

3. None of the professors at Cerebral College has ever voted Republican; therefore, well-educated people are Democrats.

The reasoning used in the passage above is most similar to that found in which of the following?

A. None of the workers in the assembly line are males; therefore, the company discriminates against men.
B. None of the keepers at the zoo have had a raise in salary for six months; therefore, the keepers are not doing their jobs well.
C. No athletes ever eat junk food; therefore, sedentary people always eat candy bars.
D. No artist buys his own supplies; therefore, all artists are supported by patrons.
E. None of the singers at the opera are female; therefore, all good singers are males.

4. No one in this whole school likes me very much. I didn't get a single vote in the last student council election.

Which of the following, if true, would most weaken the conclusion given above?

A. No one knew the speaker was running for a position in the last election.
B. The winner was elected unanimously at the last student council election.
C. Very few students bothered to vote in the last election.
D. Most of the faculty and administration supported the eventual winner of the last election.
E. The students usually vote for the most popular students.

5. Mrs. Pane was running late for work and left the house so precipitously that she left the water running and all the lights on.

Which of the following may you assume from the passage above?

A. Leaving water running and the lights on can be expensive if done regularly.
B. Mrs. Pane thought it was important not to be late.
C. Mrs. Pane was afraid to be late, fearing she might be fired.
D. Mrs. Pane was habitually late for work.
E. Mrs. Pane is not a good organizer of her time.

6. When Cressida was awarded the Manager of the Month plaque, she stated, "I couldn't have done it without my staff, all of whom I hired and trained myself."

Cressida's statement is an example of which of the following?

A. indirect self-praise
B. ingratitude

C. assuming facts not in evidence
D. a false conclusion
E. restating the obvious

    7.   Little Miss Muffet sat on a tuffet
Eating her curds and whey.
Along came a spider and sat down beside her
And frightened Miss Muffet away.

If the information above is a true account of an event, which of the following may be used as a headline that summarizes the facts without adding to them?

A. Vegetarian Frightened by Animal
B. Timorous Lady Loses Lunch
C. Spider Makes Lunchtime Advances to Charming Young Lady
D. Lady's Repast Interrupted by Spider
E. Brazen Spider Risks All for Food

    8.   No one is safe from burglars anymore. Recent surveys show that 45% of all burglary victims are big, strong men.

The argument in the passage above assumes which of the following?

  I. Most burglary victims fight back.
 II. Burglars only rob women as a rule.
III. Burglary is on the upswing in America.

    A. I only
    B. II only
    C. III only
    D. I, II
    E. None of the above

    9.   The biggest movie stars in Hollywood all revere director Li Yong; therefore, director Li Yong is the best director in the world.

The reasoning in which of the following is most like the reasoning used in the sentence above?

A. All taxpayers like to save money; therefore, an accountant who can help them pay less in taxes will be in demand nationwide.
B. The top models in Paris all like the work of photographer Scavullo; therefore, Scavullo is the world's finest photographer.
C. Professor Martinez is the most interesting professor in America today; all the Rhodes scholars try to take his classes.
D. The Pulitzer Prize was voted to Mr. Karl this year; therefore, Mr. Karl is convinced he is the best writer in the world.
E. The American runner won the 100-yard dash in the Olympics; the triumph allows him to be called "The Fastest Man on Earth."

10. All characters in Cohen's plays are Jewish. Pearl is Jewish.

Which of the following is the best conclusion to the argument above?

A. Therefore, Pearl is a character in Cohen's plays.
B. Therefore, Pearl is not a character in Cohen's plays.
C. Therefore, Pearl may or may not be a character in Cohen's plays.
D. Therefore, Pearl is the main character in Cohen's plays.
E. Therefore, Cohen's plays are all about Pearl.

ANSWER KEY

1. C	4. A	7. D	10. C
2. B	5. B	8. B	
3. E	6. A	9. B	

Explanations

1. **(C)** The key to this question was understanding the *order* of the statements. First, examples were given; then a deduction was

made based on those examples. The examples were that specific men were popular and that they were on the football team; the deduction is that by being on the football team, one may become popular. Remember: It is wholly irrelevant whether the conclusion is valid or invalid, logical or illogical. You have only to find the *form* of reasoning the writer used.

2. **(B)** This was a rather devious question. You were asked which was the *most* logical inference to draw. While almost all of the statements could be inferred (although E would be stretching it a little bit), the most logical inference is that Jacob *thought* Jake's tutoring made the difference in his grades. You cannot assume that the tutoring in fact did help Jake; perhaps his extra studying on his own, his increased maturity, or any of a dozen other factors helped improve his grades. However, because of the fact that Jacob is going to go so far as to dip into his savings just to get the same tutor, you may infer that Jacob felt the tutor made the difference.

3. **(E)** To answer a reasoning question, first identify the form of reasoning in the original passage. Here, the reasoning is that because the leaders in their field (professors at a college) don't do something (i.e., vote Republican), all persons in that field (all well-educated persons) do the opposite (vote Democratic rather than Republican). Answer E has the same reasoning. Because the leaders in the field (the opera singers) aren't something (aren't female), all of the persons in that field (all good singers) are the opposite (are males).

4. **(A)** Before you can determine which statement would weaken the conclusion, you must be certain that you have identified the conclusion. Here, the conclusion is that no one in the school likes the speaker very much. The best answer is A; if no one knew the speaker was running for office, then the fact that no one voted for him was an indication of the students' ignorance, not of his unpopularity. Answer C is close, but is not as strong. Even if only a few students voted, no one voted for him, allowing him to think he was unpopular. Answer D is irrelevant. Note that answers B and E actually *strengthen* the con-

clusion. If the winner were elected unanimously, and if the winner is usually the most popular person in school, then the speaker may have cause to believe he is not too popular. Be very careful on these strengthening/weakening questions not to choose the "opposite" answers, an answer that strengthens when the question calls for an answer that weakens, or vice versa.

5. **(B)** If Mrs. Pane left so fast that she didn't even turn off the water or the lights, then being on time must have been important to her, more important than checking the water and lights. Note that answer A may be correct in real life, but is not a valid inference based on the scant information given in the passage. Answers C and D make you infer too much; you go too far if you attribute fear or habitual lateness to poor Mrs. Pane based only on this one example. Answer E is too broad and should not be inferred from this information. In questions asking for an inference, be careful not to infer too much; use the facts of the passage and "read between the lines," but do not project qualities onto a person unless they are obviously deserved.

6. **(A)** Cressida managed to congratulate herself under a cover of false modesty. She pretended to thank her staff, but made it perfectly clear that the staff was a creation of her own. Therefore, she is praising herself indirectly.

7. **(D)** This type of question was not covered in the general discussion preceding this exam. These "headline" questions do not occur frequently, but have been seen on a few exams. Therefore, you should be familiar with them. With a headline question, you are usually given a nursery rhyme or some other little poem and asked to choose a headline that summarizes the action without adding facts not given. Usually, these answers are found via a process of elimination. Eliminate the answers that give *too much* information. Answer A gives too much; you cannot assume that Miss Muffet is a vegetarian simply because one day she was eating dairy foods. Answer B is vague; you are not told that she "lost" her lunch, only that she was frightened away. Perhaps she took her lunch with her. Answer C is hu-

morous but definitely too broad; no one knows that the spider "made advances," or that little Miss Muffet is in fact a charming lady. Answer E is also vague; what was the spider risking? You can't assume, either, that he visited Miss Muffet for the food. Therefore, by process of elimination, answer D is the best. It simply states that a lady's mealtime was disturbed by a spider—exactly what the rhyme says.

8. **(B)** First, identify the argument or the conclusion: no one is safe from burglars anymore. The writer buttresses this statement with a fact that 45% of the victims are big, strong men. You may therefore assume that the writer is rather shocked that burglars pick on big, strong men, so that "no one" is safe. Since you may make that inference, it is reasonable to think that the author has a basic assumption that women are generally the targets of the burglars, not "big, strong men." Answers I and III are too broad. You may have been tempted by answer III; however, you *know* that II is correct, and there is no answer with II and III. Besides, you cannot infer that the author thinks burglary is on the increase in America; perhaps he is lamenting the fact that it has been rampant for so long.

9. **(B)** First, identify the form of reasoning used. The writer is saying that since important people in a particular field like one person, that person must be the best in his field. Answer B uses similar reasoning. The models in Paris may be assumed to be some of the best in the world (just as actors in Hollywood may be assumed to be some of the best in the world). If they like a person, that person must be the best in his field. Note that answer C is devious; the reasoning is correct, but is *backwards.*

10. **(C)** Just because all characters in Cohen's plays are Jewish, does not mean all Jewish persons are characters in Cohen's plays. Pearl is Jewish; she may or may *not* be in Cohen's plays. Note that there could be a variation on this question. The second sentence might have read, "Pearl is a character in Cohen's plays." Then your conclusion would have been that Pearl must be Jewish. Be careful with these types of conclusion problems; do not read them backwards. Try to think of an

exception to a rule. If you can think of even one exception, do not choose "is" or "must be," but rather "may or may not be."

SCORE: NUMBER RIGHT:

NO PENALTY FOR WRONG ANSWERS

Hour Two: Analytical Reasoning

Set Your Clock. *You should have spent the first hour of today's study time learning about and practicing the logical reasoning questions. This second hour will be spent on the second type of question found in the "Analytical Ability" section, analytical reasoning.*

The Question Style

Analytical reasoning questions consist of two parts. First, you will see a set of about three to seven statements. These statements (also known as conditions) describe the structure of the relationship between items or people. Second, you will see at least three (usually more) questions pertaining to the structure of the relationship derived from the statements or conditions given. All questions in a set will refer to the same relationship; however, each question may be answered independently of the others. That is, if you cannot answer the first question in the set, do not automatically assume you cannot answer any question and skip that set entirely. No question depends on a previous question, only on the set of statements or conditions.

For the analytical reasoning questions, you may find it helpful to make a drawing, some sort of chart or table. However, doing so is not always necessary. Many people find that they can determine the relationship among the items or people in their minds and do not have to do any "artwork." Even if you do draw a chart, do not assume that there is one perfect way to do so. Although there will be one correct structure of relationship, you may derive that structure in a number of ways. For example, you may create a table while another person makes a graph. Both of you could be correct.

There are many different types of analytical reasoning questions you may encounter. (More information on these different types will be offered later in this section.) Generally, the style is as follows:

> Six students took a midterm exam.
> Paul scored three points higher than his friend Frank.

Tom scored the lowest of everyone, a full four points below Edward who was second only to Paul.

Raul studied with both Edward and Frank and got a score that was the average of their two scores.

Carl got a score four points lower than the highest score.

If Tom got an 89 on the exam, what was Edward's score?

A. 89   D. 96
B. 92   E. 98
C. 93

NOTE: More questions pertaining to the information given above would follow. Generally, there are three to six questions for each set of statements or conditions.

Format

The entire analytical ability section of the GRE consists of 25 questions which you are to answer in 30 minutes. Usually, 15 to 19 of those questions are analytical reasoning, while the remaining questions are logical reasoning. There is no special order in which the two question styles are presented (although any questions pertaining to a given set of statements will follow immediately after those statements). Unlike the math section, in which it is customary to have all the quantitative comparison questions given first, followed by all of the problem solving questions, the analytical reasoning and logical reasoning questions are mixed together.

The Basic Analytical Reasoning Questions

While there are many variations on these styles, there are five standard types of analytical reasoning questions. Each of these questions is actually a set of statements and a set of questions. These five are discussed in detail below.

1. Membership

A membership question gives you information about a group and asks you which persons or items are members of that group. For example, you may be told that Mr. Jones is a redhead while Mrs. Jones is a blonde. Next, you are informed that only blondes can join the Loyal Order of Giraffes. You now have two "deductions": first, that Mr. Jones is *not* a member (because he does not meet the membership criterion) and that Mrs. Jones may or may not be a member. Mrs. Jones does indeed meet the criterion; however, you are not told that *all* blondes are members of the group, only that in order to be a member, one must be a blonde. Generally, you will be given a specific group (schoolteachers at school X, a club or fraternity/sorority, a guest list for a party) and a list of people. Then you will be given information about the requirements for membership in the group. Last, you will be given information about the people. You are to match the requirements with the information about the people to determine who must be in the group, who cannot be in the group, and who may or may not be in the group.

When you are doing this type of problem, isolate the two distinct factors: membership requirements and personal information. Try the following example.

Club Feline is seeking new membership. In order to have your cat become a member of this prestigious club, you must have owned the cat for at least ⅔ of its lifetime. The cat must be female and must have given birth to at least two litters in the past five years.

Tabby is a male brown and white cat who has sired a litter a year for the past three years.

Calico is a female cat who has never given birth but is currently pregnant.

Snowdrop was bought by her owner eight years ago, shortly after her birth.

Princess, bought by Mr. Jones last year, has given birth to three litters in the past eight years.

1. Which of the following must be a true statement about Princess?

A. She may join the club because she has given birth to three litters in the past eight years.
B. She may not join the club because she has not given birth to two litters in the past five years.
C. She may join the club because she is female.
D. She may not join the club because she is a mixed breed.
E. She may not join the club because she has not been owned by the same person for at least ⅔ of her life.

ANALYSIS: You *may* have wanted to make a little list of notes to yourself. You may have written, "Requirements: ⅔ lifetime, same owner, female, minimum 2 litters past 5 years." If you did not want to rewrite all of this information, you could have saved time by circling it in the first paragraph. You have now done half of the analysis; you have determined what a cat must have or be or do in order to join the club. Your next step is to see whether each cat matches the requirements. Be careful to see that *all* requirements are fulfilled. If a cat matches two out of three, she still will not be given membership.

Since the question only asks about Princess, you need only focus on her. First, you are told she is a female (the pronoun "her" is used, and you are told she gave birth). You are told she has had three litters in the past eight years. You do not know, therefore, whether or not she has fulfilled the requirement of two itters in the past five years. You must leave this requirement blank unless you are given more information. Finally, you know that Princess has *not* been owned by Mr. Jones for at least ⅔ of her lifetime, since she was bought only a year ago by him. Princess must be at least eight years old since she has given birth to the litters "in the past eight years." So you summarize as follows: Princess definitely meets one criterion, being female. Princess may or may not meet another criterion, giving birth to two litters in the past five years. And Princess does not meet the last criterion, being owned by her current owner for at least ⅔ of her life.

Now, you have the harder task of answering the question. You are asked which must be true. Only the final statement, E, *must* be true. Answer B may be true—but you just don't know. Maybe at least two of those five litters were in the past five years, maybe they weren't. So statement B may be true, but is *not* necessarily true.

If you tried to be devious, and thought, "Well, Mr. Jones might have owned Princess before, then sold her, then bought her back, making him her owner for ⅔ of her life," you made matters more complicated than they needed to be. Educational Testing Service (ETS) states very specifically that in this section, no traps are intended. Read all the information and conditions and interpret them based on common sense.

There would, of course, be more questions in this set. You will have a representative sample later in the practice exam.

2. Spatial Order

A spatial order problem is probably the easiest type you will encounter. Spatial means "in space"; spatial order simply means the position of items or people. In other words, who is to the right or left of, in front of or behind, above or below (taller than or shorter than), whom. You may have all sorts of variations (who lives to the south of whom, etc.), but the means of working the problem remain the same. Try the following example:

> The librarian wants to arrange five books on a shelf according to their height. She will begin with the tallest book and go to the shortest book. The five books are A, B, C, D, and E.
> Book C is shorter than book D but taller than book E.
> Book A is the second shortest book.
> Book D is taller than all books except book B.

Which of the following represents the order of the books, from shortest to tallest?

A. A,B,C,D,E
B. B,D,C,A,E
C. E,A,C,D,B
D. B,D,A,E,C
E. C,A,E,D,B

ANALYSIS: You are told that book C is shorter than book D. Therefore, you must put C below D, as shown. Do not put C directly below D; there may be another book or books between them. Just get a feeling of the relative positions.

Fig. 1

D

C

That same sentence tells you that book C is taller than book E. Therefore, put E somewhere below C, as shown.

Fig. 2

D

C

E

The second sentence tells you that A is the second shortest book. You can't do anything with that information just yet; leave it until later.

The final sentence tells you that D is taller than all the books *except* B. This means that B *must be* the tallest book (put it at the top of your drawing) and book D must be the second tallest book. Your drawing should now look like the one in the figure.

Fig. 3

B

D

C

E

Go back to the second statement. You know that A must be the *second* shortest book. That means it cannot be the shortest; something must be below it. You know that B and D are secure in their positions; only C or E could be below A. Since E must be below C, the final order must be B-D-C-A-E.

Fig. 4

B

D

C

A

E

Now, go to the question. If you answered B, you *misread* the question. The question wants to know what the order is from the shortest to the tallest (even though the librarian, and hence your diagram, goes from the tallest to the shortest). The shortest to the tallest is E-A-C-D-B. You will often find that the question asks for an order that is somewhat unusual, such as from right to left (when we normally read from left to right). Be on the lookout for such questions.

3. Family Relationship

You may be given a problem with family members. You will be told who is the cousin of whom, who is the aunt of whom, etc. You will have to figure out the relationship among all the people, then answer questions based on those relationships. Try the following example:

L is the father of O who is the niece of Q.
P is the husband of Q and the father of M.
N is married to M.

Which of the following is a true statement?

A. P is the father of N.
B. O and M are cousins.
C. L is the father of M.
D. M is female.
E. L is the grandfather of N.

ANALYSIS: You won't want to draw an exact chart, but rather some notes to yourself. Since L is a father, he is male, He is the father of O, giving you the drawing as shown. O is the niece of Q, such that O is female. Make a line from O to Q as shown. Do not assume L and Q are siblings; L and Q could be *married* to people who are siblings.

Fig. 1

Since P is the husband of Q, P is male and Q is female. P is the father of M; you do *not* know M's gender. Since O is the niece of Q and P is married to Q, O is also the niece of P.

Fig. 2

The last sentence tells you that N and M are married; however, you do not know the gender of either.

Fig. 3

M——N
(?)   (?)

This is *all* the work you should have done on the information given. Until you have to find out more, do as little as possible. Otherwise, you may find yourself figuring out all sorts of relationships and permutations, only to discover they are never asked about.

The answer to the question is B. O and M are cousins. This is because O is the niece of Q and M is the child of Q, and they are therefore cousins.

Each of the other answers is incorrect. P is not the father of N; he is the *father-in-law* of N, since N is married to M, the child of P and his wife Q.

L is not the father of M. L is the *uncle* of M. M is the child of P, who is married to Q.

M may or may *not* be female. M could be female or male. You are only told that M is the child of P and is married to N. Since you don't know N's gender, you don't know M's gender, either.

Answer E is the easiest to eliminate. L is not the grandfather of anyone; this relationship only goes through two generations, parents and children. Grandparents and grandchildren are not mentioned anywhere.

4. Order in Time

This relationship is not too different from the spatial order. Instead of determining the position of items or people, you determine the time of occurrence of events. In other words, did A happen before or after B? Was C prior to D? Try the following example.

> Five friends are giving book reports in a class. Only one person gives a report at a time, but all five eventually give their reports.
>
> Isaac has a fear of speaking and refuses to be first.
> Gerald and Harvey are best friends and insist on speaking one right after the other.
> Joshua is ready to speak and goes first.
> Gerald speaks right after Isaac.

In which position could Karla speak?

   I. first
  II. second
 III. third
 IV. fourth
  V. fifth

A. I or II
B. II or III
C. II or V
D. III or V
E. I or V

ANALYSIS: This is a good problem to draw a chart with. First you are told that Isaac won't speak first, but note that later you are told that Joshua *is* first. Therefore, you put J at the top of your list. The first statement is *irrelevant*. It is highly likely that you would be asked a question such as "Which statement was unnecessary?" Your answer would be the first statement, since if Joshua goes first, Isaac couldn't go first. His fear of speaking makes no difference.

Next, you know that Gerald and Harvey must speak one right after another, such that you have either G, H or H, G. You do not yet know what order they speak in, nor do you know where they are in the lineup.

You are told that Gerald speaks right after Isaac. This means that your order must be I-G-H (G must go between I and H). Now you have a diagram as shown, with J on the top, and I-G-H *somewhere* below it. You do not know where K goes. She could go between J and the I-G-H, such that Karla speaks second. Or, she could go at the very end, so that Karla speaks in the fifth position. Therefore, your answer is that K could be in position two or five.

Fig. I

J

K

I

G

H

or

J

I

G

H

K

It is not uncommon to have a chart with one person or item "floating." That is, one person or item could be in one spot or another. The questions usually reflect this "float," asking you where the person *could* be.

5. Cause and Effect.

The cause and effect questions give you specific restrictions. You may be told, for example, that A can happen only if B does not happen, and that C and D must happen together or not at all. In other words, you are given a cause and asked what the possible effects are. Try the following example:

Four children are going to the doctor to get their booster shots.

Quincy will not go in the same car as Sheila because Sheila is a crybaby.

Tammy will go only if she can sit on Ricky's lap during the ride.

Ricky will only ride with Quincy if Tammy is in the car.

If Sheila is in the car, which of the following is true?

A. Tammy and Ricky could be in the car.
B. Ricky and Quincy could be in the car.
C. Quincy and Tammy could be in the car.
D. Tammy, Ricky, and Quincy could be in the car.
E. No one else could be in the car.

ANALYSIS: You have four people, Sheila, Quincy, Tammy, and Ricky. Quincy and Sheila *cannot* ride together under any circumstances; they are mutually exclusive. This is the best, most solid piece of information you have. You know now that anytime you see Quincy, you cannot have Sheila and vice versa.

Tammy won't go without Ricky—but Ricky *might* go without Tammy. Don't be confused and think that just because A must always have an accompanying B, B must always have an accompanying A.

Ricky will ride with Quincy only if Tammy *is* in the car. This means that Ricky cannot ride with Quincy but without Tammy. Note that he may ride with Tammy but without Quincy.

Now to the question. If Sheila is in the car, you know Quincy *cannot* be in that car, regardless of who the other passengers are. Therefore, you may immediately eliminate answers B, C, and D (you may often find on these types of questions that one solid piece of information helps you eliminate two, three, or even four answers right away). Now, you only have to determine whether Tammy and Ricky could ride with Sheila. The problem has no restrictions on Sheila, other than the fact she and Quincy can't be together. She could be with Tammy, as long as Ricky was there too, because Tammy won't go without Ricky. Therefore, answer A is the correct answer.

Summary. With any analytical reasoning question, take the time to determine with whom or what you are dealing (persons, things) and what type of relationship you are determining for those persons or things (spatial order? time? membership? family relationship? cause and effect?) Draw a chart or diagram *if* you think one will help you. You may wish to skim through the questions first to see whether such a chart would be useful, or would merely waste your time. If you find that you cannot create a chart, don't automatically skip all the questions. You will often be able to eliminate obviously wrong answers and make a good guess.

Traps to Avoid

1. *Do not start making notes, writing lists of people and conditions, or assembling tables, until and unless you know that doing so would help you.* Often a complete graph has much extraneous information on it.

Look at the questions first to determine the usefulness of any "artwork."

2. *Note what the question is calling for.* You may find that you created a line of people from the most to the least intelligent, only to get a question that asks you for the order of people from the least to the most intelligent. Be certain that you don't get the chart right, only to get the question wrong.

3. *Read all the answer choices.* You may think that you have the correct answer, only to find an answer later that says "all of the above." It is relatively common on these types of questions to have a distinction between what *must* be true and what *may be* true. Usually, more things *may* be true than *must* be true, allowing you to choose an answer such as "A, B, and C" or "I, II, and V." Don't be in such a rush to get through the problems that you choose the first "right" answer and go on.

Time-saving Suggestions

1. *Do all the logical reasoning questions first.* As you learned before, logical reasoning questions are sprinkled among the analytical reasoning questions in this section. Because the logical reasoning questions are generally easier to read and understand and quicker to answer than the analytical reasoning questions, try doing them first. Just be careful not to lose your place on your answer grid when you skip around within a section.

2. *Preview all the questions.* You will probably find that you are better at some types of analytical reasoning questions than others. For example, you may find the family relationship questions impossible, but the spatial order ones a breeze. If this is so, you will want to take the time to glance quickly through all the statements or sets of conditions, so that you know the style of each set. Usually, a few seconds will allow you to determine that this relationship will be one of cause and effect, while that one is membership, or something else. Do the questions you are best at first; save the others for last. That way, if you don't finish on time, the questions you didn't answer were the ones you didn't think you would do too well on anyway.

3. *Guess, guess, guess.* There is (how many times have you read this by now?) no penalty for guessing. Many people find that they have serious time problems in the analytical ability section, because of all the thinking and drawing required by the relatively sophisticated analytical reasoning questions. If you know that you are working slowly, be certain to keep one eye on the clock. When your time is almost up, fill in the blanks with some answer, any answer. If you fill in the blanks, you at least have a one in five chance of getting the question right—it's better than nothing.

Practice Exam: Analytical Reasoning

Please take the following practice exam on the analytical reasoning portion of the "Analytical Ability" section. As you learned earlier, the *whole* Analytical Ability section has 25 questions; 15 to 19 of those are analytical reasoning with the rest being logical reasoning. You have already taken a practice exam with 10 logical reasoning questions; the following exam features 15 analytical reasoning questions. An answer key and explanatory answers follow the exam. Score yourself, giving yourself one point for each correct answer. Do *not* subtract points for wrong answers.

NOTE: Since the logical reasoning and analytical reasoning questions are intermingled in the analytical ability section of the actual exam, the directions are the same for both question types.

DIRECTIONS: Each question or set of questions below is based on a short passage or upon a set of conditions given. You may draw a diagram or chart to help you answer some questions. Choose the best answer for each question. Circle the letter that appears before your choice.

Questions 1–5

Five leading sports figures are giving speeches at the Sports Convention. All five must be seated at a long table at the head of the room.

I. The tennis player will not sit next to the weight lifter.

II. The golfer must have two seats between him and the runner, because the runner smokes.

III. The swimmer is a friend of both the tennis player and the runner and must sit between them.

IV. The tennis player is seated in the second chair from the left.

1. Which of the following is the correct order in which the sports figures will be seated, from left to right?

   A. tennis player, runner, weight lifter, golfer, swimmer
   B. swimmer, tennis player, golfer, runner, weight lifter
   C. golfer, tennis player, swimmer, runner, weight lifter
   D. runner, tennis player, weight lifter, golfer, swimmer
   E. weight lifter, tennis player, golfer, swimmer, runner

2. If another chair were put at an end of the table for an additional sports figure (a polo player), which of the following could be true?

   A. She would sit four places to the left of the weight lifter.
   B. She would sit three places to the right of the runner.
   C. She would sit between the golfer and the tennis player.
   D. She would sit five places to the right of the golfer.
   E. She would sit two places to the left of the swimmer.

3. Which of the statements given above was unnecessary for your creation of a seating diagram?

   A. I or II   D. IV or I
   B. II or III   E. All statements were necessary
   C. III or IV

4. If the weight lifter and the tennis player become friends again so that they no longer refuse to sit next to one another, how many additional seating arrangements could be made?

   A. 0   D. 3
   B. 1   E. 4
   C. 2

5. Which of the following will be the first speaker?

   A. golfer   D. swimmer
   B. weight lifter   E. cannot be determined
   C. tennis player

Questions 6–10

I. Lisa is married to Mark and is the grandmother of Sarah.

II. Sarah is the cousin of Dana, who is the only child of her mother's sister, Gertrude.

III. April is the aunt of Neil, who is the child of Gertrude's brother, Frank.

IV. Gertrude and April have two children altogether.

6. Assuming that all children of Lisa and Mark have been discussed above, how many children are there?

   A. 1   D. 4
   B. 2   E. 5
   C. 3

7. Assuming that all children/grandchildren were discussed above, Sarah could be the daughter of

   I. April
   II. Gertrude
   III. Frank

      A. I only
      B. II only
      C. III only
      D. I or II
      E. I or III

8. Assuming that all grandchildren were introduced in the information given above, how many grandchildren do Lisa and Mark have?

   A. 1   D. 4
   B. 2   E. 5
   C. 3

9. Which of the following must be a true statement about Dana?

   A. He is the son of Frank.
   B. He is the son of April.
   C. He is the grandson of Mark.
   D. He is the nephew of April.
   E. None of the above.

10. If another child, Xerxes, were introduced who is the great nephew of Frank, which of the following could be true?

    A. Xerxes is a child of Sarah.
    B. Xerxes is a grandchild of Mark.
    C. Xerxes is a brother of Gertrude.
    D. Xerxes is a nephew of Lisa.
    E. Xerxes is a niece of April.

Questions 11–15

In order to become a member of the local bowling club, a person must perform all of the following steps on the same day: obtain and complete an application, be interviewed by the club president, and pay the dues in person to the club cashier.

The person who gives out applications is only available on Mondays, Wednesdays, and Fridays.

Interviews are held on weekdays, except Wednesdays.

The cashier works at another job from Thursday through Sunday and is only available to receive dues Monday through Wednesday.

11. On which day could a prospective member go through all three steps to become a member?

    A. Monday   D. Thursday
    B. Tuesday   E. Friday
    C. Wednesday

12. Which of the following is a true statement?

    A. No one can become a member on Wednesday because no interviews are conducted on that day.
    B. No one can become a member on Monday because the cashier will not accept dues on that day.
    C. No one can become a member on Friday because applications cannot be picked up on that day.
    D. All of the above
    E. None of the above

13. If the cashier were willing to come in and accept dues on Thursday,

    A. prospective members could complete all three steps on that day.

    B. prospective members could complete two out of three steps on that day.

    C. prospective members could only complete one step on that day.

    D. the interviewer would not be able to work on that day.

    E. applications would be available as well on that day.

14. On which day could a member do everything but interview?

    A. Monday   D. Thursday
    B. Tuesday   E. Friday
    C. Wednesday

15. On which day could a prospective member perform the least number of tasks?

    A. Monday   D. Thursday
    B. Tuesday   E. Friday
    C. Wednesday

ANSWER KEY

1. C	5. E	9. E	13. B
2. D	6. C	10. A	14. C
3. A	7. A	11. A	15. D
4. A	8. C	12. A	

Explanatory Answers

Questions 1–5

This is a *spatial order* exercise. You have five persons, the tennis player, weight lifter, golfer, runner, and swimmer. Call them T, W, G, R, and S for convenience.

Statement 1 tells you that you cannot have TW or WT since T and W will not sit together.

Statement 2 tells you that you must have G— —R or R— —G (there must be two spaces between the persons).

Statement 3 tells you that you must have TSR or RST.

The last statement gives you a solid piece of information, allowing you to put T in the second chair from the left.

Now that you know that T is in the second chair, you know that you must have TSR in chairs 2, 3, and 4. You cannot have RST, since there is only *one* seat before T, not two seats.

Only seats one (next to T) and five (next to R) are empty. Now, you can complete your diagram using one of two statements.

If you use statement 1, you know that T cannot sit next to W. Therefore, W cannot be in seat one; he must be in seat five. This leaves only G to go in seat one.

If you use statement 2, you know that there must be two spaces between R and G. Since R is in seat four, G must be in seat one. (There could not be two spaces between G and R if G were in seat five.)

NOTE: You could find the position of G using *either* statement 1 or statement 2, so that one of those statements alone is sufficient and one is unnecessary. You may often find on the GRE that unnecessary information is given and that you later have a question asking which statement was unnecessary.

Your final seating arrangement is G-T-S-R-W.

1. **(C)** Once you have done the steps above, you need only look at your diagram to find the right answer. Note that *this* time the question asks you for the "normal" order, left to right. Be on your guard for questions that ask you for an answer from right to left, opposite from the way most people read their diagrams.

2. **(D)** If an additional chair were added for the polo player, she would have to sit at the end of the table, either on the left next to the golfer, or on the right, next to the weight lifter. Simply go through *each* answer carefully, noting where it would place P. Answer A would have P in the seat already filled by G. Answer B would have P too far away from the runner; there would have to be an empty seat between her and W. Answer C is incorrect; there is no seat between G and T. You are told that P must sit at the end of the table. Answer D is right; five places to the right of G puts P at the far right side of the table, next to

W. Answer E is wrong; the space two seats to the left of the swimmer is already filled by G. NOTE: If you have your diagram right, questions such as this are very simple to answer.

3. **(A)** You really already answered this when you made your original diagram. You noted that you could use either statement 1 or statement 2 to fill seats one and five, so that one of those two statements is superfluous.

4. **(A)** This was rather a devious question and certainly the most difficult in this set. If W and T no longer refuse to sit next to one another, then statement 1 is eliminated. However, you have already determined that statement 1 was unnecessary. Since it is unnecessary (statement 2 still tells you that G must be in seat one and W in seat five), the patching up of the feud is irrelevant. No new seating arrangements are possible.

5. **(E)** This is a typical "trick" question. The diagram *only* tells you who sits where, not who speaks when. Do not read more into your diagram than is there. Just because one speaker sits to the right of another, does not mean he speaks before another. You have no information on the speaking order.

Questions 6–10

This is a family relationship question. Your diagram should look something like a family tree, with branches or levels for the different generations.

Lisa and Mark are the grandparents. Put them on the first level, at the top of the diagram. Since Sarah is their grandchild, put her in level 3. Be certain to leave space for a level between 1 and 3, where Lisa and Mark's child and Sarah's mother will go.

Fig. 1

1.   L—M

2. - - - - - -

3.   S

Statement 2 tells you that Sarah and Dana are cousins, so that Dana is also a grandchild of Lisa and Mark and must go on level 3. Do not put Sarah and Dana under the same parents. They are cousins, which means that their parents are siblings, not that they are siblings themselves. Dana is the only child of Sarah's mother's sister, Gertrude. This means that Gertrude is the mother of Dana. Gertrude goes on level 2, as she is the child of Lisa and Mark.

Fig. 2

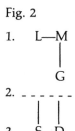

You still don't know who Sarah's mother is.

Statement 3 tells you that Neil is the child of Frank, who is Gertrude's brother. This means that Frank is on level 2 with Neil directly below him on level 3. Frank is the child of Lisa and Mark. Since April is the aunt of Neil, she must be the sister of both Gertrude and Frank.

Fig. 3

```
1.    L—M
      ┌─┬─┐
2.  (A) G  F
      │  │  │
3.    S  D  N
```

Statement 4 tells you that Gertrude and April have two children altogether. Gertrude is the mother of Dana; April must be the mother of Sarah.

Fig. 4

1. L—M

2. A G F

3. S D N

6. **(C)** The children of Lisa and Mark are on the second level. There are three of them: April, Gertrude, and Frank.

7. **(A)** Sarah could only be the daughter of April. She cannot be the daughter of Gertrude, because Sarah is the *cousin* of Gertrude's child, Dana. Sarah cannot be the child of Frank, because then April would have no children. You know that April must have one child, because she and Gertrude together have two children. Since Gertrude only has one child, April must have the other child.

8. **(C)** Look at your diagram at level 3 to see that there are three grandchildren: Sarah, Dana, and Neil.

9. **(E)** This is a rather difficult concept. You don't know Dana's gender. Nowhere are you told anything about Dana other than that (s)he is Gertrude's child. You don't know whether Dana is male or female; therefore, you can't determine whether Dana is a nephew or a niece, a son or a daughter, a grandson or a granddaughter. The question asks which *must* be true; none of the answers *must* be true. (Whenever you see the word "must" you should take note. Often many things could be true, but don't necessarily have to be true.)

10. **(A)** Frank is on level 2. His nephew would be on level 3; his *great nephew* would be on level 4. To be on level 4, a person has to be a child of either Sarah, Dana, or Neil, the persons on level 3. Since Neil is the child of Frank, Neil's child would be Frank's grandchild, not Frank's great nephew. Therefore, Xerxes would be the child of either Sarah or Dana.

Questions 11–15

This is a type of modified membership exercise where you should draw a calendar. Since only the weekdays are discussed, you can limit it to Monday through Friday.

First, you are told that to be a member, you must do *all* three tasks on the *same* day. Then you are told what the tasks are: picking up an application, going through an interview, and paying dues.

You are told that applications are given out on M, W, and F—put "app" in the spaces under those days.

You are told that interviews are held on weekdays, except Wednesdays. Put "int" in the spaces below M, T, Th, and F.

You are told that the cashier will only take the dues from Monday through Wednesday. Put "dues" in the spaces below M, T, and W.

Your completed calendar should look like the one in the figure.

M	T	W	TH	F
App.		App.		App.
Int.	Int.		Int.	Int.
Dues	Dues	Dues		

11. **(A)** A quick glance at your calendar allows you to note that on Monday, a person could get an application, be interviewed, and pay his dues.

12. **(A)** Look at your calendar to see that no one can become a member on W because no interviews are held that day. The other answers are tricky. Answer B is wrong; Monday is, in fact, the only day on which one *may* become a member. Answer C is half right and half wrong; no one may become a member on that day, but only because the cashier won't collect the dues, not because no applications are available that day.

13. **(B)** If the cashier came in on Thursday, you would write "dues" in the space under Th. This would mean that a member could perform two tasks on that day: interviewing and paying dues.

14. **(C)** Look at your chart. On Wednesday, a member may pick up an application and pay dues, but not interview.

15. **(D)** On Thursday, a prospective member may only do one thing, interview. Note that even if you "outsmarted" yourself and thought that Saturday and Sunday would be correct because nothing is done on those days, you wasted your time. Saturday and Sunday are not answer choices.

SCORE: NUMBER RIGHT:

NO PENALTY FOR WRONG ANSWERS

STUDY CALENDAR

10-HOUR STUDY SCHEDULE

	DAY 1	DAY 2	DAY 3	DAY 4	DAY 5
HOUR ONE	Suggested: Introduction and GRE Overview Completed: TIME:	Suggested: Verbal Ability (Part II) Completed: TIME:	Suggested: Math Review (Part II) Completed: TIME:	Suggested: Problem Solving Completed: TIME:	Suggested: Logical Reasoning Completed: TIME:
HOUR TWO	Suggested: Verbal Ability (Part I) Completed: TIME:	Suggested: Math Review (Part I) Completed: TIME:	Suggested: Quantitative Comparisons Completed: TIME:	Suggested: Data Interpretation Completed: TIME:	Suggested: Analytical Reasoning Completed: TIME: